Changin' Your Game Plan

R. Kearse

The Blueprint for
SUCCESSFUL Prison Reentry

"This step by step guide to helping incarcerated and formerly incarcerated individuals achieve success in their lives is remarkable. Anyone that has just a tiny bit of motivation can grow and benefit from this workbook." **DB Bedford, iNeverWorry www.ineverworry.com**

"A much needed resource for those exiting prison. It provides a powerful resource for self-examination and positive change." **Senior Government Public Affairs Specialist**

"If this workbook had of been out two years ago my brother would have been saved. He had been released from prison for only nine months and he relocated back to his childhood area and was murdered. I always prayed for a program such as this for my brother, and other family members to be able to have, as a tool to begin a journey of successful reentry back into society. This workbook is just like creating a business plan for your life. **Natasha Harris-Foster, Broken Wings Literacy Center**

"Changin' Your Game Plan is your exit strategy out of a lifestyle that has taken more than it has given." **Jm Benjamin, Bestselling Author, (formerly incarcerated)**

"This was an excellent ass book excuse my French but I read the book before my release and it helped me in a major major way. I'll be receiving a state proclamation on the 20th of July from the state of Pa, that book was definitely a stepping stone for myself." **Amber L. Sloan, Founder of M.A.D.E. I.T (formerly incarcerated)**

"This workbook can help the millions of men and women who are currently incarcerated or under some sort of court ordered supervision." **Anthony McFadden, Reentry Specialist**

"This will definitely help increase a person's chance of making a successful transition back to society, his/her community and family (short term goal) and staying out of prison (long term goal)." **Daniel Gonzalez, Business Owner (formerly incarcerated)**

"If you want your incarcerated love one to change, give him/her a point from where to start from. Changin' Your Game Plan provides that starting point. This workbook is an investment in their future." **Ahmed Dickerson, Father of Formerly Incarcerated Son**

Prison Statistics

- The average age of released prisoners is 33 years old.
- The average education level of released prisoners is the 11th grade.
- Among those released, there is a high incidence of substance abuse, and mental, or phyical, health problems.
- Stable housing is a problem for many prisoners after release.
- Below average levels of education, work experience, or skills makes finding steady employment challenging for ex-offenders. Many employers will not hire ex offenders.
- Former prisoners are more likely to have significant mental disorders, chronic and infectious diseases, and to return to communities with inadequate health care.
- Although the majority of prisoners have had a broad history of substance abuse, less than 33% receive treatment upon release.

Source: The Urban Institute, June – 2010

- 95% of state prisoners will be released back into their communities.
- In 2008, 735,000 persons were released from state and federal prisons, a 20% increase from 2000.
- Approximately nine million people are released from jails each year in the U.S.
- In 2008, parole violations accounted for 34.2 % of all prison admissions, 36.2 % of all state prison admissions, and 8.2 % of all federal prison admissions.
- 25% of all adults who exited parole in 2008 (133,947 people) went back to prison forviola ting terms of their supervision, and 9 percent of adults were sent back for committing a new crime.
- Two out of five prison and jail inmates lack a high school diploma, or a GED.
- Employment rates and earnings of incarcerated people are often low before their incarceration due to limited education, low skill levels, physical and mental health problems, and other factors. Incarceration exacerbates these employment challenges.
- A large three-state recidivism study found that less than half of those released from prison had a secure job waiting for them when they returned home.

Source: Department of Justice Statistics – 2010

- Research by business professor Matthew Sonfield showed that those who are incarcerated have similar or higher entrepreneurial aptitude than various other types of entrepreneurs.

- Women comprise seven percent of the state prison population, but are the fastest growing portion of the incarceration population Source: Harrison and Black - 2006

- In 1980 the U.S. imprisoned 12,331 women in state correctional facilities. That number jumped to 98,602 by 2005, an increase of nearly 700 percent.

Source: Bureau of Justice Statistics - 2005

Forward  by Terence Jeffries, Founder; City of Refuge Ministry

"The real fight isn't in the cage, it is the weight cut, the time you put in at the gym. Wining a fight is your payout from all the hard work you put in." - *MMA fighter Corie Hoard*

Up one late night reading a book, with the TV on in the background, I overheard heard a Televangelist challenging his congregation, "Show me a successful person and I'll show you a person who purchased that success with the currency of time." Lowering the book half way down I heard him say it again, "Show me a successful person and I'll show you a person who purchased that success with the currency of time." Bending over to put the book down, I stayed in that position with my elbows on my knees and hands under my chin and like in the movie Poltergeist I was drawn into the television. The thinly built, middle-aged pastor, sweating profusely, stood angrily glaring over his congregation for almost a full minute. Pausing

another moment to wipe the sweat from his forehead and repeated himself verbatim, "Show me a successful person and I'll show you a person who purchased that success with the currency of time." I grabbed a pen and wrote those words on one of the first blank pages of the book I was reading and added my own words, "The only one who can stop me is ME!"

For the first time in my life I could honestly say that I had a clear concept of what it was going to take to create success. What the pastor was able to provide for me was, a visual formula for what it was going to take to create that success. To create success it was going to take change. Change in the way I viewed time and change in the way I used my time. The formula I envisioned looked like this: Hard Work + Sacrifice = Success. Nothing about this formula is nuance. In some way or another we've all been taught this before. I remember the saying my grandmother used when she would wake us up, "Sleep ain't nothing but a dream." Or that catchy little saying your grade school teacher would plant in your head, "A stitch in time saves nine" and "Don't put off for tomorrow, what you can do today." In none of these sayings is the word "time" ever mentioned, but if one is paying close attention he or she could only come away with a renewed value of its worth.

September 13, 1999, I was sentenced to serve 130 months in federal prison. At 33 years of age, my life to that point had been a mixture of highs and lows. When I say a mix of highs and lows, I really mean a mix. There was a period in my early life when all I ever thought about was being a police officer. I slowly turned from that dream and focused on a career as a lawyer. I enrolled in John Jay College of Criminal Justice and was on my way. After almost two years at the city college I followed a few of my friends to Shaw University in Raleigh, NC. I was pursuing my dreams and the future was bright, but just like texting while driving, things can change quick-fast-in-a-hurry. Instead of staying on the path leading me toward success, I made a wrong turn and headed down south on the road toward self-destruction. That road would eventually end with me spending a 10-year vacation at club fed, also known as Federal Prison.

When you're on the road heading toward self-destruction you don't realize where that road is taking you because you're too busy enjoying the ride. You're in the driver's seat and your vehicle's name is *Life*. Driving *Life* full speed ahead, you're oblivious to the warning signals meant to slow you down and get you back on the road towards success. It's not until you run out of gas, when you realize you're somewhere you don't want to be and you're not the driver you thought you were.

The sad and unfortunate thing is, given the opportunity to map out a new course and choose a different destination many individuals will choose to get back on the road to self- destruction as soon as they can drive their vehicle called *Life* again.

Thirty-three and looking at forty-three upon my release, I knew something had to change.

Giving my life to Christ had freed me internally, but all the external evils and distractions still existed. The biggest of them all was idleness. I see idleness as a shopping mall where more impulse buying takes place than any other mall in the world, and what always happens is, we wind up over-spending for worthless pleasures. Think about the one-hour after breakfast you spent talking about the game last night. The two hours a day you spend talking about what you used to have. The four-six-eight hours a day you spend watching television. The one-hour a day you spend arguing about nothing. The time you spend with people you know don't want to change. Get the picture? Do you see how much TIME we SPEND on NOTHING? How much TIME we WASTE? Would you pay $2000 for a $500 car or a $1,000 for a $5.00 pair of shoes? I don't think so, but in all actuality this is what most people do in prison on a regular basis. Is this you?

Chances are, if you're reading this book right now you're in the market for change. I have good news and bad news for you. The bad news is; change is going to cost you. The good news is; you have the currency to pay for it... TIME!

The odds are, most of you have failed to use your time wisely and as a result you find yourself facing some difficult challenges ahead. If you're not prepared to meet those challenges the repercussions will be severe and in some cases prove to be fatal. A volunteer who spoke to us at Federal Prison Camp Jesup some years ago made it even clearer, "If you don't take TIME to work on creating the life you want, you're eventually going to spend a lot of time dealing with the life you don't want." With recidivism numbers going through the roof and college grads fighting for the same jobs as ex-felons, the writing is on the wall: "Change now or pay for it even more later."

Randy Kearse has put together a workbook that brings together all the tools one will need to have in place to live a positive and productive life beyond the barbwire fences of America's penal institutions. The Changin' Your Game Plan: The Blueprint for SUCCESSFUL Prison Reentry, is all about change. A major emphasis is placed on time, the one commodity that every inmate across America is rich in but fails to spend wisely. Randy Kearse, ex-felon turned author, film producer, motivational speaker, and Life Coach attributes most, if not all, of his success to careful preparation during his thirteen years of incarceration. Constantly repeating in his workshops, "If you fail to plan, you plan to fail." This workbook will assist any serious minded individual ready for change and preparing for success. Let these words serve as motivation as you prepare to be transformed by the renewing of your mind.

How to use Workbook

To get the most of this workbook follow the following guidelines:

➤ If using as part of a group, don't read ahead of the group.
➤ If using on your own, find someone who can go through the workbook with you.
➤ Use with an open mind, honest heart and it will you give you the power to change.
➤ Read each chapter thoroughly and let the words marinate.
➤ In the chapters you find vocabulary words in bold, look up the word in the back of the workbook to help you better understand each chapter and grow your vocabulary. Take the time to look up and learn these words and any others you may not know.
➤ Definitions are in the context of how the word is being used in the chapter.
➤ Think about how the chapter relates to you and what the author was trying to express.
➤ After you read each chapter, review and answer the discussion questions that correspond to that specific chapter.
➤ Discuss your answers and thoughts with the group (or with a friend/family member if you are studying this workbook individually).

➤ During discussions listen and respond respectfully to other people.
➤ Don't turn discussions into debates.
➤ Be mindful that everyone doesn't see things the same. Experiences, cultures and other factors help shape our perspectives, views and opinions.
➤ At the end of most chapters and question sections, there's a Chapter Afterthought for you to assess what you got out of the chapter.
➤ Finally, at the end of the workbook, there are pages where you can map out your new game plan.
➤ Use the blank pages at the very back of the book to make notes, jot down your thoughts and/or keep track of information that can be helpful to you.

When you complete this workbook program there's no certificate, no graduation and no early release from prison. This isn't that type of program. The rewards you will receive come long after you have completed the workbook program if you utilize the lessons properly. Completing the program is just the first steps in the journey to reclaim your life, your respect and your place in the world. The real test comes when you have to practice and apply all the things you have learned about yourself effectively, it is only when you reach that point in your life that you have accomplished your goals, been mentally and physically free from prison for years at a time, will you have graduated to a better life.

What is the purpose of the workbook?

_____

_____

_____

_____

Why is changing your game plan important?

_____

_____

_____

_____

How can you turn your incarceration into a learning experience?

_____

_____

_____

_____

How does being in prison make you feel?

_____

_____

_____

_____

What is more productive, discussion or debate?

_____

_____

_____

_____

Table of Contents

From The Author

My name is Randy Kearse. I'm an author, publisher, host and producer of "Straight Talk w/Randy Kearse." I'm a filmmaker, motivational speaker, and entrepreneur. I'm the guy who wrote the critically acclaimed book *Changin' Your Game Plan: How I used incarceration as a stepping stone for SUCCESS*. Before I was any of those things, I was just like you, sitting in prison trying to figure out what my next step in life was going to be. I had 15 long years to think about it. One thing I was certain of, if nothing else, I was not coming back to prison. I started writing *Changin' Your Game Plan* during my 15-year federal prison sentence and finished it on the streets.

Changin' Your Game Plan is about my life, experiences, overcoming adversity, the challenge to change, and how I took a negative situation and turned it into a positive opportunity. I created this workbook, *Changin' Your Game Plan: The Blueprint for SUCCESSFUL Prison Reentry* to help people just like you, who are incarcerated, formerly incarcerated or headed to prison formulate a positive game plan for their life.

I remember many days during my incarceration when me and a few other guys would gather together and *"build"* on the yard, in the library, or in the chapel about doing something positive with our lives during and after our incarceration. When I say *"build"*, I mean we would have deep philosophical discussions about life. We discussed everything; politics, religion, the streets, the street and prison mentality, the choices that landed us in prison, relationships, and many other things. There was no right or wrong during these discussions, because the purpose of *"buildin"* was to examine, explore, and expand our perspectives, as well as engage in critical thinking. I have had some of my best thought-provoking discussions in prison. So with all that said, one of the underlining purposes of this workbook is to get you to think, change, and prepare for the future.

Have you ever asked yourself why so many people return to prison? I asked myself this question on numerous occasions during my 15-year prison sentence, and in a quest to find the answers that would keep me from coming back, I wrote *Changin' Your Game Plan: How I used incarceration as a stepping stone for SUCCESS*.

The most important question you'll be faced with during your incarceration is, do I accept and embrace change or do I refuse and reject it? During my incarceration I faced, fought, and overcame many battles raging inside me; conflicting battles of beliefs, mindsets, morals, values, and accountability. Change wasn't easy, and it darn sure didn't happen overnight. It was a process. It was something I worked on every day. As time went by, change became a part of me, it became what I stood for and the guidelines I would live my life by.

This powerful workbook is a blueprint for successful transition back to your family, community, and ultimately, back to your life. It provides you with the tools, resources, and confidence you can use to stay out of prison.

My proven method of change is changing the hearts, minds and futures of the most hardened street individuals. Rising from the ashes of poor choices, bad decisions, and a destructive lifestyle, I'm living proof you can go from being a statistic to being a success.

Standing in a room full of currently incarcerated men, I often ask this question, *"what if I had a way for you to leave prison right now, how many of you would take it? Be honest, raise your hands"*, I tell the men. Hands slowly begin to rise, as the men start to comment. "Darn right", "Who wouldn't want to leave this miserable God forsaken place?" "Absolutely", are a few printable responses I hear. *"Now that I have their full attention"*, I say, *"that's what got a lot us of in prison in the first place, "instant gratification", wanting the things we want when we want them instead of working towards earning the things we want."*

Most people wanna go from Point A to Point Z without going through the rest of the alphabet. The journey to your new life is just as an important as reaching the destination. The lessons you will learn along the way will be priceless. I can't begin to tell you how my prison experience and the lessons I learned from it have added such depth to my life.

Some of you will be tempted to read though this workbook in a few days, looking for that "quick fix" or those proverbial "secrets to success" we always hear so much about, while some of you will take your time and pour over every word, pick apart every lesson to be learned, collect every jewel dropped in this workbook. Whether you use this workbook on your own or as part of a group, the only way to truly get the most of it is by approaching it very methodically. Rushing through this workbook will defeat the main purpose of what it was intended to do, help you create a new game plan for your life.

Now is the time to decide whether to be active in our own life and future or stand on the sidelines being silent, letting others pretty much make the choices for you. When you are active in your own life, you are the Commander-and-Chief of your future. You get to decide if you're satisfied with the direction your life has been going in or whether it's time to take your life in a bold new direction.

My mind opened up, my perspective broadened, and I learned so much *"building"* with guys during my incarceration. I'm sure our discussion would rival any of the ancient philosophers you read about in books today. I can hear echoes of "Yoooo that's deep" or "Yoooo that was deep son" in my ears as I write this. Creating this workbook took me back to those days on the yard and how charged I felt after a "building" session. I know a lot of you are hungry for change, but please don't try and devour this workbook in one or two sittings. Take your time and slowly digest each word in each chapter, answer each question only after seriously pondering an answer that is truly reflective of your feelings. Make notes to yourself. I did my best to arm you with all the tools you will need to keep you out here, when your bid is over. Ten years from now when someone asks you how you managed to stay out of prison, just say, "I decided to Change My Game Plan."

Introduction

Most people don't wake up one day and decide they want to go to prison. Prison is usually the **consequence** of embracing negative morals, values and principles, engaging in a destructive lifestyle and buying into a mindset that accepts prison and death as the ultimate sacrifice to the so-called game. Before most people get physically incarcerated they have been brainwashed and incarcerated mentally.

Changin' Your Game Plan: The Blueprint to SUCCESSFUL Prison Reentry is a **practical** approach to change, doing your time, and successfully transitioning back to your family, community and life in a positive productive way. Just because some of your past poor choices have put you in the situation you are in, doesn't mean you can't begin to make better choices right now (in the present), choices that will keep you out of the criminal justice system. Use this time to take stock of your life and ask yourself, *"Where am I, how did I get here, and what do I need to do to move forward?"*

Your *game plan* is the goals and plans you make for your life. Your past game plan obviously hasn't yielded positive results, so now it's time to rip it up, trash it and begin from scratch to create a new game plan you can win with.

> *"I was mentally incarcerated for 15 years (from the age of 15/16 until I was 30/31), I was physically incarcerated for close to 15 years of my life and I was street incarcerated (under supervised release) for 10 years. You do the math"*, Randy says.

Changing your thinking, behaviors, and attitudes are part of the process to creating a new game plan. By changing your *game plan,* you will greatly increase your chances of not only successfully **transitioning** back to society, but also increase your chances of staying out or prison.

The author of this workbook, Randy Kearse, has successfully mapped a way out of the negative mindsets and behavioral patterns which send so many people back and forth to prison. Spending more than 30 years of his life incarcerated in one shape, form or fashion, Mr. Kearse lived a similar lifestyle as you, but broke free from the mental incarceration that led to his physical incarceration.

Changin' Your Game Plan is not based on prison reentry theory or on a set of thoughtless ideas developed by a nameless official tucked away in a comfortable office somewhere, who doesn't have a clue what the day to day struggles are for someone who is not only getting out of prison physically, but, someone who has to breakout of the mental prison he or she has been living in for some almost half their life.

Changin' Your Game Plan is based on tried and true methods of change created by Randy Kearse, someone who has *walked the yard*, spent months at a time in *the hole*, and done time in half a dozen prisons during his 15-year Federal prison sentence.

Randy will be the first to admit that taking his life from a negative to a positive was not easy to do, and far from simple. In the end he will also tell you it was all worth it. Randy knew his **resolve** to change would be challenged on so many levels when he was released from prison, but he was determined to prove the changes he made while incarcerated were now the foundation in which he planned to live his life. Change while in the penitentiary was a great start for Randy, but he knew before he could write about change, he had to live it and be an example of it.

By taking the necessary steps to change you gain the power to create a positive game plan for your life. You don't have to wait until you are physically free to take control of your life, because once you make the decision to change you begin taking back control of your life.

Trying to rebuild your life after prison can seem like an insurmountable task for many people, that's why it's imperative you prepare for your future now instead of trying to figure it out 90 days before your release date, like a lot of people do. When someone asks you, "What are you going to do when you get out", you want to have a solid answer (your action plan) in place, opposed to answering, "I'm a see when I get out there."

The challenges you face are many and **complex**. But they are not impossible to overcome. This workbook will help you distance yourself from the negative mindsets, values, and principles you adopted on the streets. It will help you embrace the concept of change as you construct a new game plan for your life after prison, probation and/or parole.

Changin' Your Game Plan: The Blueprint to SUCCESSFUL Prison Reentry will help you peel back the layers of the old you (like the layers of an onion) and show you how to rebuild (a positive mindset), re-construct (a positive value system) and re-invent yourself (based on positive principles and codes of conduct).

Time doesn't stop because you're locked up. Time is your life and how you spend your time will determine what kind of life you will have after prison. Going to prison wasn't part of your old game plan, but staying out of prison has to be an important piece of your new one.

What can you expect to get out of this workbook?

- ✓ Personal Growth
- ✓ Self-Awareness
- ✓ Critical Thinking Skills
- ✓ Self Esteem Building
- ✓ Attitude Adjustment
- ✓ Anger Management
- ✓ Problem Solving
- ✓ Relationship Building
- ✓ Presentation Skills
- ✓ Vocabulary Building

Mere possession of this workbook will cause people to look at you differently. Some people will be supportive of you and your willingness to entertain change and some people will try to discourage you by making light of what this workbook represents. Before you even get into using it you will be faced with your first change challenge. It will be that some of the people you associate with who will fire the first salvo of discouragement. Some will say, "*I don't need to change my game plan*", when they eye the title to the workbook, and some will say things like, "*I already have a game plan*", or "*that book ain't gonna change you.*" Be mindful, when you make a decision to do something different with your life, not everybody will be supportive of you. That will be one of the prices you pay when you stop trying to fit in and live a life that stands out

How did I wind up here? (In prison)

_____

_____

_____

Where do I go from here?

_____

_____

_____

What do I want to accomplish during my incarceration?

_____

_____

_____

How will prison change me?

_____

_____

_____

How can I make this time work for me?

_____

_____

_____

How will my incarceration define me?

_____

_____

_____

Looking back at your life, list 3 *if I would of, could of, should of* moments.

Moment #1

1. If I would of _____

    _____

2. I could of _____

    _____

3. I should of _____

    _____

Moment #2

1. If I would of _____

    _____

2. I could of _____

    _____

3. I should of _____

    _____

Moment #3

1. If I would of _____

    _____

2. I could of _____

    _____

3. I should of _____

    _____

Author's Biography

Born and raised in the Farragut housing projects in Fort Greene, Brooklyn, Randy Kearse had many opportunities growing up. He came from a loving nurturing family where he learned positive values. He was a straight A student until the 10th grade when he became bored with school and dropped out. He began getting into trouble, and was arrested at 17 for attempted murder. Adjudicated a youthful offender, Randy was sentenced to 6 months in jail and 5 years of probation; he spent his 18th birthday behind bars. By the time he was 21, Randy's life was fully **entrenched** in a cycle of drug dealing, violence, and crime.

Before Randy became the infamous street pharmacist known on the streets of Brooklyn to the streets of three cities in North Carolina, he was just a **scraggly** little kid growing up with more options in life than most kids were getting in Brooklyn at the time. It was in the mid 1980's the very early days of what would later be called the crack epidemic, and now known as the crack era when Randy jumped head first into the **vile** world of the drug trade. The so-called game became his life, the only thing he lived to do. He traded in his childhood dreams, for the dream of being a successful drug lord. Randy switched friends who lived the straight and narrow, for the grimy, untrustworthy, and shady characters you run with in the streets.

For the love of the money he became enemies with childhood friends and **forged** alliances with people he had little or no history with. He would achieve a level of success in the drug world that many lesser drug dealers could only dream about. At 26 years old, Randy was arrested and indicted on a **slew** of federal offenses including drug trafficking and weapons possession. He was found guilty and sentenced to 15 years in federal prison, not before the sentencing judge called him a menace to society.

Randy's life isn't the kind of story based on poverty, a **dysfunctional** family or having a lack of opportunity. No, it's a story about someone who had every opportunity in life to become whatever he wanted to become, but instead chose the bright lights of the streets and the street fame that came with it. It's not an easy story to tell, filled with heartache, pain, and suffering. He caused a lot of hurt to others and to himself. His story is also about **redemption**, overcoming **adversity** and the challenge to change. It's a testimony to the strength of the human spirit and how God's plan moves all of us through the good, the bad, and the ugly.

During his long years of incarceration Randy went back to the one thing he truly loved, writing. Not even people close to him knew he had a secret passion for the written word, or that he penned his first novel at 19 years old. With no knowledge of how to pursue his dream of being a writer back then, Randy ditched his writing dream and succumbed to the street life.

August 2015 makes ten years since Randy walked out of prison with nothing more than two manuscripts, a plan and a strong determination to never return. Using prison as a constant reminder, he regularly tells himself, *"no matter how tough it gets out here, it can be a lot worse if I slips up."* With the whole ten years spent on supervised release, Randy knows he was always one bad choice away from going back to prison.

Randy attributes his successful transition back to society, his family and community to the work he did on himself and the vision he created while in prison. Randy sums it like this, *"I had a choice, become a better criminal or a better individual."*

What is a Biography (Bio)?

_____

_____

_____

What can we learn from a person's Bio?

_____

_____

_____

_____

What were you thinking as you read Randy's Bio?

_____

_____

_____

_____

What stood out to you in Randy's biography? Why?

_____

_____

_____

_____

Did anything surprise you about Randy's Bio?

_____

_____

_____

Was there anything in Randy's Bio that you can relate to in your own life?

_____

_____

_____

_____

Write a short description of 3 people's bios you are familiar with.

1. _____

_____

2. _____

_____

3. _____

_____

List 3 bad decisions you've made in your life?

1. _____

_____

2. _____

_____

3. _____

_____

What is a eulogy?

_____

_____

_____

_____

Write a Bio (Biography) about yourself.

Preparing For Success

During my incarceration I would hear guys complain day in and day out about everything under the sun when it came to being in prison. You name it, guys complained about it. The amazing thing is, even with all the complaints people have about their confinement, bad food, lack of privacy, mistreatment, lack of adequate medical attention and more, the rate of people returning to prison is **staggering**. Some statistics show close to 62 percent of people released from prison will return to prison within 3 years. This is outrageous! How come so many people who have been subjected to such inhumane treatment and **degradation** return to prison in such a short period of time or return to prison at all?

The truth is, most people who are incarcerated fail to prepare for the future. People go through the motions of time without taking the time to make the necessary changes that will keep them from returning to prison.

Preparation is the one and only thing that can increase a person's chances of not returning to prison. Without proper preparation people go back out to society with the same negative mindset, destructive behavioral patterns, and street schemes they had prior to their incarceration. Think of preparation as an **investment** in your future. The more you prepare, the better chances of you getting a return on your investment. The rewards you get from your investment are many; a positive future, a new lease on life, and peace of mind. Peace of mind is a place in your mind where there's no stress, no worries, no doubts, and no distractions.

The Five Ps

- Proper
- Preparation
- Prevents
- Poor
- Performance

There's a right way and wrong way to prepare for your future. The right way is to use the time you have POSITIVELY and PRODUCTIVELY in PREPARATION of your release. Preparing will increase your chances of STAYING OUT. The wrong way is to do nothing with your time and that will most definitely increase your chances of returning to prison. Failing to prepare, is preparing to fail.

Properly preparing for your release will take work. You have to get mentally, physically and emotionally prepared for the challenges ahead. There are several challenges you have to prepare for in order to have a smooth and successful transition.

Rejection; within society, from family and friends. Practicing patience. Attitude. Focus. Presentation. Falling back into negative habits, thinking, behaviors, and more. How you respond to these challenges will determine if you stay out of prison or return.

Keep in mind you're not just preparing to get out of prison, noooo, it's much much deeper then that. You are preparing for your life. Long after you get out of prison you will have to go on with the business of living your life. Everything you do or don't do from this point on to better yourself will have a direct impact on your life way after you leave prison. Getting out of prison is just half the **equation**, staying out is the other half.

An Athlete doesn't prepare for just one game, he/she spends countless hours, days, months and sometimes years practicing and honing their skills. He/she knows in odered to win a championship; you first have win a series of games. In order to win a championship the athlete knows he/she has to be, focused, disciplined, committed, dedicated! Right now you're training to be a champion in life. I'm giving you the blueprint to step your game plan up to compete on champion status. It is now up you, to take that blueprint and run with it. The Five's Ps lay it out for you plain and simple.

Most people who have successfully transitioned from prison back to society usually have one thing in common.... They took the time to work on themselves while inside and left prison with a plan.

For the people using their time in prison to strengthen criminal ties, learn new criminal schemes or dreaming about returning to their criminal ways upon release, you are preparing to fail. If you spend your time gangbanging, drug dealing, becoming a prison celebrity, involved in prison politics and indulging in all the **frivolous** things that go on in prison, you are preparing to fail.

You do not get to choose where you are right now, but you do get to choose where you want to go and the life you want to lead when you get out. The decisions you make today will help decide your fate tomorrow. Preparation is critical to your success; it's perhaps the most valuable component. You can dream about being successful, or you can wake up everyday and work hard toward it. If an opportunity presents itself and you're unprepared, chances are the opportunity will pass you by.

If you can prepare for your immediate needs like housing, employment, medical, and government assistance before you are released that will be less pressure on you to figure it out when you actually get released. Gather all the information you can that will direct you to the resources available for people getting out of prison. Reach out to reentry programs in your area about your needs prior to being released.

Though you can't prepare for every unseen obstacle, challenge, or situation you will be faced with upon your release, you can surely use the time you have to run through numerous **hypothetical** situation drills to mentally prepare for what lies ahead of you. Assess your daily routine and ask yourself, are you doing the things that will help you or hurt you when you get out. If you're spending more time and energy on things that can't help you, then you are preparing to fail.

There is no secret to success. Successful people will tell you what it took for them to be successful and there are thousands upon thousands of books, videos, and audiotapes that explain what it takes to be successful. Success is the destination but the journey to get there takes a lot of hard work, patience, preparation, discipline, consistency, determination, and an absolute unshakeable belief in what one is striving to do. Stay the course even when success seems so far away it feels unreachable. Ignore people when they try to tell you your dreams are unattainable. Push yourself day after day, week after week, month after month and year after year to be the best at whatever you want to do and be in life.

How do you define failure?

_____

_____

_____

How do you define success?

_____

_____

_____

If you are doing these things in prison you are preparing to fail.

➢ _____   ➢ _____

➢ _____   ➢ _____

➢ _____   ➢ _____

If you are doing these in prison you are preparing for success.

✂ _____   ✂ _____

✂ _____   ✂ _____

✂ _____   ✂ _____

What should you have in order before leaving prison?

1. _____

2. _____

3. _____

4. _____

5. _____

6. _____

List reasons people return to prison.

  ✂ _____   ✂ _____

  ✂ _____   ✂ _____

  ✂ _____   ✂ _____

List excuses people give for returning to prison.

  ✂ _____   ✂ _____

  ✂ _____   ✂ _____

  ✂ _____   ✂ _____

What are some reasons people manage to stay of prison?

  ✂ _____   ✂ _____

  ✂ _____   ✂ _____

  ✂ _____   ✂ _____

Is there a difference between *being ready to go home* and *being prepared to go home*?

When you are *ready* to go home _____

_____

_____

When you are *prepared* to go home_____

_____

_____

How can you tell someone is ready and/or prepared to leave prison?

_____

_____

_____

If you were released from prison tomorrow, can you honestly say you are mentally and emotionally ready to leave? Explain why or why not.

_____

_____

_____

_____

When you see someone return to prison, how does that make you feel?

_____

_____

_____

_____

Write a sentence for each of the Five Ps.

1. _____

2. _____

3. _____

4. _____

5. _____

What are some other "P's" that will help you be successful?

✂ _____

✂ _____

✂ _____

✂ _____

✂ _____

Chapter afterthoughts

What did I get out of this chapter?

_____

_____

_____

_____

How can I apply this chapter to my life?

_____

_____

_____

What will I do differently now?

_____

_____

_____

What questions should have been asked in this chapter?

✂ _____

✂ _____

✂ _____

What can I add to this chapter to make it more powerful, engaging or helpful?

_____

_____

_____

_____

_____

_____

What is Change?

Before you get started, let's discuss CHANGE. What exactly is Change? What is the process of Change? How do we measure Change? Should we ever stop **striving** for Change? Is Change even Possible? These are just some of the questions you should ask yourself as you move forward and embark on your journey of change. Change is the process of becoming different. It's important because it helps us learn who we are, the world we live in, and what our purpose for living is. In order to survive every living thing has to change eventually.

You've already experienced change in your life once before, but it was probably so long ago you've forgotten when or how it even happened. Think back to a time before you began to make poor choices, got involved in the streets, started using drugs, stealing etc. (In the 'hood we say "when you started coming out the house.") The change you experienced then was negative, it happened over time, and when enough time passed, your negative changes overshadowed the positive parts of who you really are. You embraced the negative changes and made those changes a part of how you wanted the world to see you.

Change isn't always pretty. Some people will openly embrace it, some people will run from it, others will have to be dragged kicking and screaming towards it and some will rather die before they try it. There are times when positive change is born out of the worst **circumstances**. But the underlying basis for change is often the need to better one's situation. Change can bring you face-to-face with your own personal truth and offers 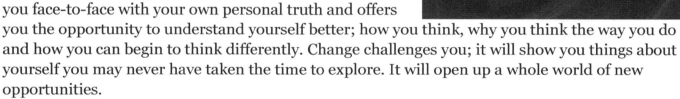 you the opportunity to understand yourself better; how you think, why you think the way you do and how you can begin to think differently. Change challenges you; it will show you things about yourself you may never have taken the time to explore. It will open up a whole world of new opportunities.

Is change difficult? For a lot of people it is. The fear of change is the biggest reason why so many people resist change. Many people fear a new way of thinking or doing things. They fear not being accepted by family, friends or peers. The fear of leaving ones negative COMFORT ZONE makes many people **resistant** to change. Inside your negative comfort zone you feel safe, hiding behind your negative thoughts and behaviors. You can do wrong for so long it stops feeling wrong. Many people live in denial of their need to change. Some people want to change but lack the know-how, tools, or confidence it takes to change.

How do you get past the fear of change? The first and most important step is to **acknowledge** there is a need to change. The next step is FACING YOUR FEARS. Once you face your fears you have a chance to explore where your fears stem from, what **triggers** them, and how to manage them. Change is a process, it's not something that will happen overnight. If you embrace change and respect the process of change your chances of making positive changes in your life greatly increase. Each step of this workbook walks you through the process of change. You can judge your success by looking at the **gap** between where you are, where you used to be, and where you want to be. This perspective helps you figure out what remains to be done, when you look at the progress you've made over a course of weeks, months, and years.

How do you define change?

_____

_____

_____

How do you measure change?

_____

_____

_____

List and explain 3 reasons why people resist change?

    1. _____

    2. _____

    3. _____

Do you believe you can change? Yes [ ] No [ ] Explain

_____

_____

_____

List 3 changes you need to make in your life and why?

    1. _____

    2. _____

    3. _____

What are 3 benefits of change and why are they beneficial?

    1. _____

    2. _____

    3. _____

What are 3 consequences of rejecting change?

1. _____

2. _____

3. _____

Why is change a slow process?

_____

_____

_____

Why do some people struggle with change?

_____

_____

_____

Why is change necessary for survival?

_____

_____

_____

Name 3 people you know who have changed and how each one has changed.

Ex: My friend John. He used to do drugs and now he's been clean a year and telling young people about the dangers of drugs.

1. _____

_____

2. _____

_____

3. _____

_____

Are you ready for change? Why/Why Not?

_____

_____

_____

Can you believe in yourself even if no else one does? Yes [ ] No [ ]

_____

_____

_____

Name 3 things that change on the outside while a person is in prison.

    1. _____

    2. _____

    3. _____

When is change a bad thing?

_____

_____

_____

In order for a person to change he/she has to do what first? Explain

_____

_____

_____

What don't some people want/like to see other people change for the better?

_____

_____

_____

Chapter afterthoughts

What did I get out of this chapter?

_____

_____

_____

_____

How can I apply this chapter to my life?

_____

_____

_____

What will I do differently now?

_____

_____

_____

What questions should have been asked in this chapter?

✂ _____

✂ _____

✂ _____

What can I add to this chapter to make it more powerful, engaging or helpful?

_____

_____

_____

_____

_____

Sailing

I got to get my Ship Right... Start SAILING upstream far away from those who refuse to dream.

TIME to SAIL forward and beyond YESTERDAY.

I got to fix this Ship from Top to Bottom because the WATERS of LIFE have WRECKED many of my UNPREPARED SHIPS BEFORE.

Kept them in the dark and in the docks of procrastination while SAILING in circles...

I got to get my Ship Right... Saw too many Shipwrecks that didn't have to be, didn't have to float in the Dead Sea of Drugs and Other Deadly Vices.

Saw too many Ships float endlessly and aimlessly without emotions or drive, without concern or care fueling their journey.

I saw too many Ships SINK in the Waters of stubbornness, unhappiness, no faith, and no goals...

I got to get My Ship Right... Fulfill GOD'S purpose, satisfy my own self-worth, TEACH my people, REACH my people.

I got to follow MY OWN HEART, MY OWN MIND and TRUST that GOD IS ORDERING MY STEPS!

I am SAILING on the RIVER BANKS of LIFE being fueled by the SACRED BLOOD of ANCESTORS whose stories MUST BE TOLD WHOLE!!!

I got to get My Ship Right and steer myself to the Shores of Tranquility.

How is YOUR SHIP DOING? What kind of waters YOU SAILING IN?

Why is "Sailing" a great title for this poem?

_____

_____

_____

What is the message in the poem?

_____

_____

_____

What makes this poem so important?

_____

_____

_____

What part(s) of the poem can you relate to?

_____

_____

_____

Does this poem make you think about the direction your life is or has been sailing?

_____

_____

_____

Can you think of 3 other titles for this poem?

1. _____

2. _____

3. _____

Write a poem about your life. Include the past, present and future (as you see it).

Chapter afterthoughts

What did I get out of this chapter?

_____

_____

_____

_____

How can I apply this chapter to my life?

_____

_____

_____

What will I do differently now?

_____

_____

_____

What questions should have been asked in this chapter?

✂ _____

✂ _____

✂ _____

What can I add to this chapter to make it more powerful, engaging or helpful?

_____

_____

_____

_____

_____

Examine the Front Cover

Pictures are worth a thousand words. When you pick up a book the first thing you see is the cover, the cover is supposed to "speak to you" so you can get an idea of what the book is about before opening it.

Does the cover of this workbook "speak to you?" and if so what is it saying, and if not why not?

_____

_____

_____

_____

Why do you think Randy Kearse chose this picture for the cover of this workbook?

_____

_____

_____

_____

Why do you think Randy didn't show the face of the man holding the handcuffs? And should he have?

_____

_____

_____

Why is the man dangling the handcuffs on one finger?

_____

_____

_____

_____

Table of Contents

Take a look at the table of contents on pages 6. Which four chapters look the most interesting to you? Why?

Chapter title _____

_____

_____

_____

Chapter title _____

_____

_____

_____

Chapter title _____

_____

_____

_____

Chapter title _____

_____

_____

_____

_____

Create four new chapters and write two paragraphs for each as if this workbook were yours.

Chapter title _____

_____

_____

_____

_____

_____

_____

_____

_____

_____

Chapter title _____

_____

_____

_____

_____

_____

_____

_____

_____

_____

Chapter title _____

_____

_____

_____

_____

_____

_____

_____

_____

_____

Chapter title _____

_____

_____

_____

_____

_____

_____

_____

_____

_____

_____

The last chapter of your life's story ends with you going off to prison. How does the next chapter start?

_____

_____

_____

_____

_____

_____

_____

How would you describe your life's story so far? Explain.
Ex: Comedy, Drama, Mystery, Sci-Fi, Action

_____

_____

_____

_____

Name people who play a role in your life story and what role each plays.

_____   _____

_____   _____

_____   _____

_____   _____

_____   _____

The Journey to Self-Discovery

The day you **consciously** decide it's time to make changes in your life is the day your journey to self-discovery and to a new you begins. Facing yourself to get to the root of the issues, which have been holding you back, is a courageous undertaking, but sometimes it can be painful as well. As with any journey, it all starts with that first step. Your journey can be an **empowering** chapter in your life because the personal level of growth you will experience and achieve will feel like an **awakening,** but it won't be easy. To get the best results and reach your true potential, you will have to commit to working on yourself EVERYDAY!

The decisions you make early in your incarceration will have a strong impact on where you'll find yourself at the end of your sentence. If you get involved with all the negativity that goes on in prison the odds are, you will go through your incarceration doing nothing **constructive** or positive with your time.

Self-discovery should be an important goal of yours while incarcerated. Some people go through life playing a role and others simply become what others want them to be. Your journey will give you the courage to remove your mask and see yourself for who you really are. If you decide not to take this journey of self-discovery, you will cheat yourself out of the opportunity to understand who you are, what you want out of life, and your life's purpose. You can't leave where you are until you choose where you want to be. You have to be decisive about what kind of you future you want.

Search for something you can become **passionate** about because when you're passionate about something, it will energize you to pursue whatever that passion is. Energy is everything when it comes to being successful. Figure out what you want, and then pursue it with an unwavering passion. Eat, sleep and pursue that passion 24/7, even if isn't financially rewarding.

Life is a continuous exercise in creative problem solving, so you have put your thinking cap on tight. Make decisions instead of excuses because a mistake doesn't become a failure until you refuse to correct it. Thus, most long-term failures are the outcome of people who make excuses instead of decisions.

Your incarceration has the potential to bring out the best in you if you let it. Every true champion has to be tested, and this journey you are about to go on is part of your test. You are fighting to regain your self-respect, **dignity** and in a lot of cases to reclaim your very soul. The streets, prison, drugs, violence eventually take a toll and slowly chipped away at that positive good-hearted person that is buried inside you.

Quitters never win and winners never quit. A true champion will never bow to defeat even faced with **insurmountable** odds. A true champion will fight his/her way to victory. The judge laid you down, but you don't have to "lay down" during your incarceration, if you decide to "lie down" and do nothing to better yourself, you can't blame that on the judge. You hold the keys to what you do with your time while you are doing your time.

How do most journeys begin?

_____

_____

_____

_____

Why should a person get to know him or herself?

_____

_____

_____

_____

How do people get to know themselves?

_____

_____

_____

_____

Does the journey to self-discovery ever end?

_____

_____

_____

What is an "underdog"?

_____

_____

_____

_____

Have you ever felt like an "underdog"? When and why did you feel that way?

_____

_____

_____

_____

Why do people cheer for the "underdog"?

_____

_____

_____

_____

List 3 things it takes to be a champion?

1. _____

2. _____

3. _____

What is the best "comeback" story you have heard or personally witnessed?

_____

_____

_____

If a person gives up, quits or lies down, what does that say about him/her?

1. _____

2. _____

3. _____

4. _____

Chapter afterthoughts

What did I get out of this chapter?

_____

_____

_____

_____

How can I apply this chapter to my life?

_____

_____

_____

What will I do differently now?

_____

_____

_____

What questions should have been asked in this chapter?

- ✂ _____
- ✂ _____
- ✂ _____

What can I add to this chapter to make it more powerful, engaging or helpful?

_____

_____

_____

_____

_____

Self-Improvement

There comes a time in everyone's life when you know you're not living right. Your life is in **chaos**, you're living a destructive lifestyle and in your heart of hearts you know it's only a matter of time before your demons finally catch up to you. Prison is a like a pause button for an out of control life. In a lot of cases, prison was the last stop before a person's life crashed and burned. Now that your life is on pause, you have the opportunity to work on yourself and make some much-needed improvements. Self-improvement is just that, taking steps to improve one's self. The core of self-improvement is honesty. You have to be totally honest with yourself in order for the process to have a lasting impact on your life.

Being honest with yourself means asking the hard questions about yourself only you have the answers to. Like, (*do I really want to go back and forth to prison? Am I tired of living the way I do? Am I happy with my life up to this point? Do I really want to grow old in prison? What has been my greatest obstacle in life? Am I ready to face and deal with my* **unresolved** *issues?*)

It's hard to honestly *"evaluate"* ourselves because we're afraid of what we'll see and eventually have to admit about ourselves. The same **critical** methods we use to analyze others we need to apply to ourselves. Being able to "self-evaluate" will be a major step toward self-improvement. It's not going to be easy to put yourself under the magnifying glass and examine your flaws, but it is a necessary procedure. It's easy to point out the flaws of others, instead of trying to fix what's wrong with us. You can lie to everyone else, but you cannot lie to yourself. It takes time, honesty, and **discipline** to develop the courage and will to change.

Few skills are more important to self-improvement than being able to take a step back and honestly evaluate one's self. Self-evaluation allows you to expose your flaws, address unresolved issues, and identify **potential** stumbling blocks.

Unfortunately, honest self-evaluation is one of the hardest skills to master. People tend to be self-serving in their thoughts. For most people, self-evaluation means taking a look at in that mirror they have been painfully trying to avoid. The impact honesty will have on your self-evaluation **outweighs** the temptation to sugarcoat or downplay your flaws.

Figuring out where we are and how we got there is one goal of self-evaluation. No matter where you want to go, you must begin with where you are. And if you don't know where you are, you must begin by finding out. Self-evaluation is the process of finding out where we are and who we are at the same time.

Self-evaluation gives you the ability to **cultivate** the true potential within you. It means stripping away all the **superficial facades** and getting down to what you're really made of and the great things that you're capable of achieving. Your seriousness, your truthfulness and your determination to improve yourself will decide how powerful you become.

In order to make your self-improvement most effective you have to apply the following methods: *self-examination, self-analysis, and self-confidence.* When you apply the *self-examination*, you look at yourself and make a list of all your positives and negatives, strengths and weaknesses. Be truthful. When it comes to your positives, you want to look for ways to expand them. Your negatives, you want to look for ways to eliminate them. Your strengths, find ways to benefit from them. Weaknesses, find ways to strengthen them.

When you go in the *self-analysis* phase of self-improvement you want to analyze yourself for the purpose of better understanding you. You want to understand the reasons you think the way you do, see things the way you do, and do the things that you do. You want to get to the core of where some of your negatives and/or weaknesses stem from? You want to **analyze** the bad decisions you've made in the past to figure out what you could've done better and what you need to do to keep from making the same mistakes.

Adults normally influence how we think, rationalize, and behave during our early childhood years. These influences can be negative, positive ,or a combination of both. We can also be influenced by trauma we witnessed happening around us. In order to analyze yourself you have to travel back in time in your mind and explore who and what has had an impact on your rationale, actions, and behavior. From there, you will be able to analyze whether those influences have helped or hurt you throughout your life. Where it has hurt you, you now have the power to rid yourself of those harmful influences.

Revisiting the past is never easy, but a lot of times it's necessary in order to figure out how we can make out ourselves better. There's huge difference between dwelling on the past and revisiting the past for the purpose of self-improvement. When you dwell on the past, you are holding on to the past and the past becomes a ball-and-chain around your ankle, dragging the past around with you everywhere you go. When you revisit the past for self-improvement purposes you are examining the past looking for the keys that will unlock the ball-and-chain around your ankle. No one can change the past, but if you better understand it, the chances are you will make more informed and wiser choices in the present and in the future.

Right now your life is like the tale of an old classic car. After many years of wear, tear, and bad maintenance by the owner parts got old, worn out, and before you know it the car eventually broke down. Before the owner junks the car he/she realizes the car has value if he/she can restore the car back to its original condition. So what does the owner do, he/she sends the car to a garage so a mechanic can work on the old classic. Like the classic car, right now your life is in the garage and you're the mechanic assigned to fix and restore it. In order to do that you have to first figure what's wrong with your car (life). What parts are good, bad, worth saving, and the parts you need to trash. Now... you can be the kind of mechanic that does a lousy job, uses cheap and/or junk parts, slaps some new paint on the car and then tries to pass the car off as fixed and restored. Or you can be the kind of mechanic who takes pride in his work, spares no expense and makes sure he uses all the best parts to fix and restore his classic, because at the end of the day, your classic car (life) can look shiny and new on the outside, but it's what's under the hood that will determine the worth and value of your classic.

There is never an end to the journey of self-improvement. The more you grow, the more you realize there is *so much out there you don't know, so much that you have to learn,* and there is always something about ourselves we can improve on. The human potential is limitless, so it's impossible to reach a point of no growth. Whenever we think we are good, we can be even better.

Take an honest look at yourself and describe what you see?

_____

_____

_____

What are 3 benefits of self-improvement?

1. _____

2. _____

3. _____

Why is it so easy to find fault in others but not in our own self?

_____

_____

_____

If no one is "perfect" can we use that as an excuse when we make poor choices?

_____

_____

_____

How will you know when you've grown?

_____

_____

_____

Some of my strengths are:

✂ _____

✂ _____

✂ _____

✂ _____

Some of my weaknesses are:

✂ _____

✂ _____

✂ _____

✂ _____

Some of my positive qualities are:

- ✂ _____
- ✂ _____
- ✂ _____
- ✂ _____

Some of my negative qualities are:

- ✂ _____
- ✂ _____
- ✂ _____
- ✂ _____

Where has my negative behavior gotten me?

_____

_____

_____

Explain how your poor choices/negative behavior impacted other people.

- ✂ _____
- ✂ _____
- ✂ _____
- ✂ _____

Name the people who positively influenced your thinking, rationale or behavior throughout your life.

_____ _____ _____

_____ _____ _____

_____ _____ _____

Name the people who negatively influenced your thinking, rationale or behavior throughout your life.

_____ _____ _____

_____ _____ _____

_____ _____ _____

Chapter afterthoughts

What did I get out of this chapter?

_____

_____

_____

_____

How can I apply this chapter to my life?

_____

_____

_____

What will I do differently now?

_____

_____

_____

What questions should have been asked in this chapter?

✂ _____

✂ _____

✂ _____

What can I add to this chapter to make it more powerful, engaging or helpful?

_____

_____

_____

_____

_____

Playing the (so-called) Game

I used to think the life I was living on the streets was part of some kind of *Game*. I was *True To The Game*, I was *Game Tight*, I had *Game*, and I *Played The Game* to the fullest. I believed violence came with *The Game*, going to prison was just *Part of the Game*, and death was supposed to be *Charged to the Game*.

This was the mindset I accepted the first time I was *Introduced To The Game*. At 14-years old I got *Schooled To The Game* by my much older Uncle Bugs. Bugs literally taught my friends and me *how the game was supposed to be played*. He'd tell us all kinds of slick stuff *like game is meant to be sold – not to be told*. He told us and taught all sorts of illegal cons and hustles. When he came around he flashed wads of money and made sure he shared his wealth with us; at 14, a hundred dollars meant you were rich.

"The workingman is a sucker", Bugs would say. "I don't want nothing old, but a bankroll" was his favorite line. He wore the finest clothes had the prettiest women and was treated like a celebrity in the neighborhood. Who wouldn't want to be like Bugs? *The Game* was clearly being good to him. By the time I reached 20 I convinced myself I was *in the game*.

At 20, I was *knee deep in the game*. I thought I had all angles covered like my Uncle Bugs had taught me. You couldn't tell me I wasn't born for this lifestyle. I went to jail a few times, lost a few friends along the way, seen friends go to prison for *forever*. Seen families destroyed, dreams crushed and innocent people caught in the crossfire of violence, drugs and chaos. My Uncle never taught me about the **flipside** of the so-called *game*. As I got older I realized there was a lot of things Bugs had left out about the so-called *game,* but that wasn't until I'd been through enough to see the *so-called game* for what it really was; a bunch of bull-crap.

The Game is this **fictitious** way of living that is nothing more than an **illusion**, which allows people to justify, rationalize, and celebrate wrong. It allows those who play the so-called game to go through life without owning up to the destruction and damage they are doing to themselves and others to acquire the rewards the so-called game promises to it's players.

The truth of the matter is, there is no such thing as *"The Game"*. What we call the so-called *game* is actually life itself and life is not a game. If you continue to approach life and the decisions you make in this life as some sort of game there's only two ways the so-called game ends; prison or death.

No one is born to play the so-called *game*. We are taught to adopt the mindset and behaviors that are associated with the so-called *game*. Not everyone **gravitates** to the so-called *game*, that's why I don't buy this whole notion that people are *"Products of their Environment"*. It's my strong belief people are the *"Products of their Choices"*.

Everyone you grew up with did not go to jail/prison, sell/do drugs, carry guns, commit crime, try to solve problems with violence, or didn't become a teen parent, all the negative behaviors often associated to growing up in a particular environment.

The sooner you understand that life is not a game, the sooner you can make the changes that will alter the direction of your life. Games are supposed to fun. Where's the fun in spending 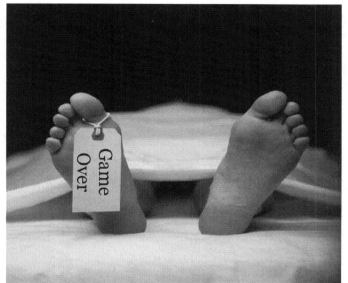 x-amount of years in prison or subjecting yourself to pain, loneliness and despair? Where is the fun in watching your children grow up in pictures? Where's the fun in being taken away from your family, friends and community?

Living life like it's some kind of game **diminishes** a person's ability to consider the real consequences of their action until their actions cause consequences that are undeniably real. The day the judge banged that gavel and gave me 15-years in prison is the day the so-called *game* got real for me. Most of the people I know who chose to better themselves during there incarceration have all said being sent to prison was a sobering wake up call for them and they no longer looked at life as a game. When you take life seriously, everything you do, you do with a purpose-driven mindset. You understand you hold the keys to your future and if you continue living life as a game you will put the keys to your future in someone else's hands.

The so-called game is smoke and mirrors used to **brainwash** people into falling in love with a lifestyle that will ultimately destroy them and potentially destroy those around them. The so-called game has been **romanticized** in films, books, and in music, but anyone who stands for truth will tell you the so-called game for all its glamor, glitter, and promise of fame is nothing more then street fairytale. There's no pot of gold at the end of the rainbow, no riding off into the sunset, and definitely no buying an island in the middle of nowhere. Half the people who play the so-called game end up broke somewhere (most likely in prison) **reminiscing** and telling tall tales about all the money they made, the women they had, cars they drove long after their run has ended. All that's left is faded memories held to together by the faded pictures in a worn torn photo album. The other half wind up dead buried and long forgotten by the same people who celebrated their street fame. And for those who don't wind up spending their later years in prison or who have barely managed to stay alive will forever be slaves to the so-called game because of their unwillingness to change.

When you finally realize this thing (*the so-called game*) is one big lie, it's like finding out the woman or man you have been in love with all these years never loved you, was lying to you, and had many other lovers the whole time. Breaking up with the so-called game will be hard for a lot of people, because they've been in love with the lie for so long. Instead of trying to make the lie work for me, like so many do, I decided to appreciate the lessons the lie taught me. You can learn something from the worst relationship and breaking up is never the end of the world, it's the beginning of a new one.

What are 3 reasons people use to justify playing the so-called *game*?

1. _____

2. _____

3. _____

Why do so many people compare life to a game?

_____

_____

_____

_____

Looking back, who or how were you *"introduced to the game"*?

_____

_____

_____

List 3 Pros of *"The Game"* and why.

1. _____

2. _____

3. _____

List 3 Cons of *"The Game"* and why.

1. _____

2. _____

3. _____

Do the Pros outweigh the Cons or visa versa? Explain

_____

_____

_____

Is the so-called *"Game"* winnable? Explain

_____

_____

_____

Does the person play *"The Game"* or does *"The Game"* end up playing the person? Explain

_____

_____

_____

What does *"Charge it to the game"* mean?

_____

_____

_____

Do you regret something you *"Charged to the game"*? Explain

_____

_____

_____

If *"the game don't stop because you locked"* when does the *game* stop?

_____

_____

_____

What have you learned from the so-called game that you can use in your new life?

_____

_____

_____

Chapter afterthoughts

What did I get out of this chapter?

_____

_____

_____

_____

How can I apply this chapter to my life?

_____

_____

_____

What will I do differently now?

_____

_____

_____

What questions should have been asked in this chapter?

✄ _____

✄ _____

✄ _____

What can I add to this chapter to make it more powerful, engaging or helpful?

_____

_____

_____

_____

_____

Mentally Incarcerated

Physical incarceration is not the only form of incarceration a person can experience. When you are physically incarcerated you can see the barbwire fences, gun towers and prison walls that hold you captive. When you are mentally incarcerated, your thoughts are locked behind the barbwire fences, gun towers, and prison walls of your mind. There are many people who have never been incarcerated physically, that are walking around mentally incarcerated.

Mental incarceration is a mindset that keeps a person locked in a negative thought process that produces no positive reward, outcome or progress. When a person is mentally incarcerated their mindset is the biggest **obstacle** to his/her own success.

People mentally incarcerated are extremely *closed-minded*. It's difficult to get them to think outside-the-box about anything. A sign of mental incarceration is when someone is unwilling to rethink his/her approach to a situation he/she never gets a positive result from; their thought process is locked up.

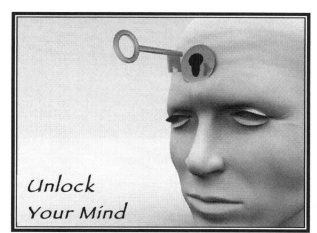

Unlock Your Mind

Finding the courage to open up your mind is how you begin to break out of mental incarceration. When you open your mind to take in new information, new experiences, and new positive people, you slowly come out of the cell you've been living in, in your mind. I became mentally incarcerated when I allowed myself to believe the only way for me to be successful was to have money and street respect. My mind was so locked up I didn't see anything wrong with selling drugs, my willing to kill, be killed or spend the rest of life in prison for the money, the false sense of power and respect, drug dealing gave me.

When a person is mentally incarcerated he/she falls victim to what I call accepted ignorance. Accepted ignorance is the mentality that keeps people from reaching their full potential because it doesn't promote positive or critical thinking. It's that mentality which makes people idolize and respect pimps, drug dealers, and gang bangers. It teaches us to take our criminal cues from images we see in movies like *Super Fly, The Mack* and later on *Scarface, King of New York* and *Good Fellas*. We watch these moves and fantasize about being a big time drug dealer or gangster.

When a person is mentally incarcerated he/she believes going to prison or dying in the streets is *part of the game*. People will say things like, *"The streets is all I know"* or *"The only thing I know how to do is hustle"* but these are only excuses used to justify continuous negative and illegal behavior. These sayings only state one's unwillingness to try or learn something different.

Rap further **exacerbates** the situation by encouraging people to live their lives according to the streets. Rappers adopted, exploited and sold people the same street life images they were getting from people like you. For the sake of making money a lot of rappers tried harder and harder to come across as being a real street dude. In doing so, rappers sold a whole generation of young people an illusion of the street life. While dudes like us were getting a hun'ned years in prison or getting killed, rappers were talking about what they were doing from the safety of a studio. With the constant bombardment of negativity, a whole generation has been **indoctrinated** in the ways of accepted ignorance. People are dying and going to prison under the guise of '*Keepin' it street, gangsta, real, and 'hood.*"

Breaking out of a mental prison isn't easy. The thought process we've been using is entrenched in our **psyche**. We allowed ourselves, in most cases to develop a **warped** sense of excuses, justifications and **rationales** for the things we did. Undoing all that is going to take some time, but for every old way of thinking you let go of, you also gain a new way of thinking; the trade off is an **exhilarating** feeling.

When you decide to break out of the mental prison of your mind, you will literally go to war with yourself. The good and bad in you will have an epic battle to determine the future direction of your life. The bad in you has been calling all the shots for so long, it will not turn over the power to make positive decisions over to the good in you so easily. The bad in you will do everything in its power to convince you not to change, it will remind you of the "fun" you've had, the "respect" you've gained, and the "love" the streets have given you. The bad in you will replay and replay old memories of all the times you felt like you were on top of the world. The good in will only have visions of what life can be if you change. He/she will ask you to trust him/her to make the right choices moving forward and this will be the struggle you will be faced with. I decided to trust the good in me because I saw the damage that bad in me had done all these years.

During my incarceration I went on what I like to call mental **pilgrimages** in search of answers that would make my life make sense. I refused to believe prison was the end of my story. In my heart of hearts I knew there were chapters of my story yet to be written and if I could step up my level of thinking, the following chapters of my life would have profound meaning. It was during these soul-searching pilgrimages I found the keys to unlock the cell doors of my mind. I began to raise my consciousness level. The opposite of being mentally incarcerated is being mentally conscious. When you become mentally conscious you become aware, more informed and get a better understanding how different issues impact you, your family, community, society, and the world.

When you begin to raise your conscious level, eventually the doors to the prison cell in your mind will have to burst open. You will begin to challenge your old way of thinking, as well as stop letting your old way of thinking dictate how you view yourself, approach situations, rationalize and justify your choices, actions, and behaviors.

Consciousness is like a drug, the more conscious you become, the more conscious you want to become. As you grow consciously you will feel a certain responsibility to enlighten and share information with other people, but keep in mind, just because you are growing consciously doesn't everyone around you or on the outside is experiencing conscious growth too. Not everyone is going to be where you are or where you want to go consciously and that can become an issue for you. There are a lot of people who don't want to be consciously awakened, who are just fine having other people doing the thinking and/or decision making for them.

Conscious people are those who are not afraid to think outside-of-the-box, refuse to take things on face value, and are willing to not only ask the hard questions, but who also spend the time searching for the answers. Just because a way of thinking is accepted as the norm, doesn't make that thinking right. There was a time, thinking the world was flat was the norm.

Define "mental incarceration."

_____

_____

_____

List words associated with a "mentally incarcerated" mindset. Ex: Stubborn

_____   _____   _____

_____   _____   _____

_____   _____   _____

List 3 examples of accepted Ignorance.

   1. _____

   2. _____

   3. _____

How can you free yourself from mental incarceration?

_____

_____

_____

What are some signs a person is "mentally incarcerated"?

_____

_____

_____

How can someone in the free world be mentally incarcerated?

_____

_____

_____

Name 3 people you know who are mentally incarcerated? Explain how.

1. _____

   _____

2. _____

   _____

3. _____

   _____

What is the opposite of being "mentally incarcerated"?

_____

_____

_____

What happens when you become conscious?

_____

_____

_____

Why is knowledge power?

_____

_____

_____

_____

Name 3 conscious people you know or heard of. What makes each one conscious?

1. _____

2. _____

3. _____

Chapter afterthoughts

What did I get out of this chapter?

_____

_____

_____

_____

How can I apply this chapter to my life?

_____

_____

_____

What will I do differently now?

_____

_____

_____

What questions should have been asked in this chapter?

✂ _____

✂ _____

✂ _____

What can I add to this chapter to make it more powerful, engaging or helpful?

_____

_____

_____

_____

_____

Institutionalized

While I was in prison we would jokingly say a guy was "institutionalized" when we'd catch him demonstrating certain repetitive behaviors. If you were one of those guys who'd sit in the same seat in the mess-hall every meal everyday, put your chair in the same spot in the day room everyday (and be ready to fight if someone had their chair there), or would practically run to the mess hall every meal, everyday to us those were signs you were *institutionalized*. I was accused of being *institutionalized* every now and then (I admit I did the mad dash to the mess hall on chicken and fish day).

As comical as it might sound, everyone in prison runs the risk of becoming institutionalized to some degree during his or her incarceration. When you have to adapt to and make adjustments in an environment that keeps you on guard 24 hours a day, 7 days a week, it makes you feel **isolated** and **devoid** of emotions or feelings. It can leave an everlasting impact on your psyche. Making a simple adjustment like eating a meal in as little as 6-minutes, done over a period of time, can become so routine you may forget it was an adjustment you made for survival purposes. The challenge you face is not allowing the adjustments you make to survive your prison experience, from becoming a permanent part of who you are.

Some will say being institutionalized is a state of mind, and on a case-by-case basis it's according to how an individual **processes** his or her prison experience. One person can leave prison after over a decade and not **exhibit** any behaviors associated with his or her incarceration, yet someone who may have been in prison a few months may go home with many of the behaviors associated with being incarcerated. Prison changes everyone no matter who it is. No person leaves prison the same as he or she went in. Only you can determine how much of an impact prison will have on you, and whether that impact will be a negative or positive one.

Tips to avoid becoming institutionalized.

- ✂ Do not let prison define you
- ✂ Do not lose your dignity
- ✂ Create positive routines
- ✂ Create positive habits
- ✂ Do not indulge in negative behaviors
- ✂ List the adjustments you made in prison
- ✂ Keep abreast of changes happening in society.

The prison environment promotes **dependency** upon policies, practices and structures over personality, empowerment, and free will. **Spontaneity** and ordinary personal interactions have all but been extracted from the prison environment. Many of the temporary adjustments you make to survive your incarceration are not adjustments you want to bring home with you.

Don't lose touch with the way life is lived in the world outside. The daily routines, the **monotony** and "doing time" coping **mechanisms** can cause you to forget you are living in a manufactured environment. Day after day, week after week, month after month, and year after year of "sameness" has the potential to erase any traces of real world normality if you let it.

What are 3 reasons people become institutionalized?

    1. _____

    2. _____

    3. _____

What are 3 signs someone is institutionalized? (Not mentioned in chapter)

    1. _____

    2. _____

    3. _____

What are 3 adjustments you had to make to survive prison?

    1. _____

    2. _____

    3. _____

What are 3 re-adjustments you will have to make when you get out of prison?

    1. _____

    2. _____

    3. _____

What are 3 feelings/emotions you have to hide while you are in prison? And why?

    1. _____

      _____

    2. _____

      _____

    3. _____

      _____

What are 3 ways your family/friends can help you readjust to being free?

1. _____

2. _____

3. _____

What are some stigmas associated with being incarcerated?

✂ _____

✂ _____

✂ _____

✂ _____

✂ _____

What 3 telltale signs someone has been or recently released from prison?

1. _____

_____

2. _____

_____

3. _____

Why do some individuals become institutionalized and some do not?

_____

_____

_____

Do you feel you are or are not institutionalized?

_____

_____

_____

Chapter afterthoughts

What did I get out of this chapter?

_____

_____

_____

_____

How can I apply this chapter to my life?

_____

_____

_____

What will I do differently now?

_____

_____

_____

What questions should have been asked in this chapter?

✄ _____

✄ _____

✄ _____

What can I add to this chapter to make it more powerful, engaging or helpful?

_____

_____

_____

_____

_____

Get Ya Mind Right

Albert Einstein said, "You cannot solve a problem with the same mind that created it."

When you walk back into the free world, you have to be mentally prepared for the road ahead of you. Even with the best-laid plans, you have to be mentally prepared to follow through with your plans. If you haven't mentally prepared yourself for all the **scenarios**, distractions and **impulses** awaiting you when you walk out of prison you're going to be **overwhelmed** with your newfound freedom to make choices again.

Getting your mind right means mentally preparing for getting out of prison. If you are easily **swayed** or influenced by the distractions on the streets you won't stand a chance. Distractions come in all shapes, sizes and forms at any given moment.

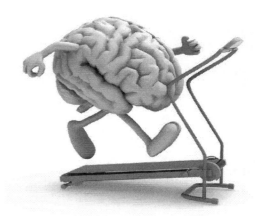

When you're mentally prepared to leave prison, you already see the big picture and you understand how important patience is to your success. You are prepared to incorporate the lessons your incarceration has taught you into your immediate, short-term, long-term and lifetime plans because you know the stakes are high.

How and what we think directly affects our moods. Very often we **sabotage** ourselves with our own unhealthy thinking. Events or situations do not determine our mood. Instead, how we think about the event or situation typically determines our mood. So if thinking affects our feelings, we can change how we feel by changing how we think.

You have been mentally poisoned and the only way to get ya mind right is to mentally **detoxify** from all the poisons that have corroded your mind; the *drugs, violence, crime, money, prison, gangs, etc.* Depending on how long your mind has been poisoned, it might take some time to get your mind right. The first step is cleansing your mind and your life of toxic people and toxic relationships that do not promote positive growth. Change your thoughts and you literally help change the world you are living in.

Reading will definitely help you get ya mind right in prison, but it's not how much you read, it's what you read that will determine how reading plays a part in your progress. If all or the majority of your reading consists of books or magazines that promote the same lifestyle you're trying to get away from, the same lifestyle that sent you to prison, the same lifestyle that sent a lot of your loved ones to the graveyard, it's going to be hard to get ya mind right, because your mind won't experience growth. Just like you have to be careful what you feed ya body, you have to be careful what you feed ya mind. The same holds true to the music you listen to, the TV you watch and the information you take in from the people around you. If all the music you listen to is negative, all the TV you watch is negative and the conversations people are having around you are negative, then you leave yourself little or no room to grow because your mind is still being fed negative information. Negativity is like having weeds in the garden of your mind, for the garden (your mind) to grow, you have to pull out all the weeds that have been destroying the garden.

To get your mind right you also have to educate yourself. Get your General Equivalency Diploma (GED), enroll in classes available and learn a trade. Furthering your education by any means will help you get ya mind right immensely. I have seen so some many men neglect to pursue even a basic education because they felt embarrassed to let other men know they had poor reading, writing, and arithmetic skills. There's no shame in having a below average education right now, the shame is in allowing what other people think about you to stop you from getting the help you need to better your education. If you don't have a GED get ya GED, take advantage of all the educational opportunities that might be available to you within the institution you are doing your time.

There are a lot of people incarcerated who still think they can get by in life on street smarts alone. Though having street smarts does have its share of advantages, having street smarts and book smarts makes a person more equipped to navigate in life spaces where having street smarts is not enough. A combination of street smarts and book smarts, enhances your life smarts.

Outside of what traditional educational opportunities are available to you in prison, you can also take time to educate yourself in various ways. You can educate yourself about people, politics, society, how local, state and federal government works, about your history and more. All learning moments are not found in a classroom. You can find a learning moment in almost everything; experiences, things you see, hear or read. Look closely enough and you can learn something around everywhere you look. You know the old saying, *"you [can] learn something everyday."* Well spend everyday learning at least one new thing, no matter how small that thing is.

People who take the initiative to educate themselves and/or teach themselves something new are said to be self-taught. Being self-taught is an outstanding achievement. People who are self-taught are generally passionate about learning new things and not discouraged by the work, discipline and determination it takes to learn something new. You are educating yourself by using this workbook. Educate yourself about the reentry process and where you can find the resources to help make your transition as smooth as possible.

When I was a young boy, my father worked at night for the NYC Transit Authority and he would come home with a newspaper every morning and in the back of the daily newspaper there would be an Asian cartoon character named Luck Eddie. Lucky Eddie would have a quote or saying everyday, so my father would call each one of children to read Lucky Eddie and then tell him (my father) what the Lucky Eddie quote meant. With this daily routine my father was teaching us how to think, and how to get meaning out of what we read. Develop the ability **interpret** (read between the lines) things when the meaning is not clearly spelled out.

Tips to Get Ya Mind Right

- **Meditate**: Meditation will give you an opportunity clear your mind of negative thoughts and replace them with positive ones.
- **Read**: Read books, newspapers and magazines which challenge you to think and/or rethink your views, opinion and perspectives about everything from health, wealth, politics, society, history, religion, life and family. (Use television for this purpose as well)
- **Music**: Listen to music with a positive message.
- **Write**: Write down positive and inspiring quotes you come across.

List 3 things you can do to "mentally prepare" for your release

1. _____
2. _____
3. _____

What are 3 signs someone is not "mentally prepared" for his/her release?

1. _____

_____

2. _____

_____

3. _____

_____

What are 3 ways you can free your mind?

1. _____
2. _____
3. _____

What kind of reading material should you read to get ya mind right?

_____

_____

_____

Does reading urban street fiction help you get ya mind right? Why/why not?

_____

_____

_____

_____

Interpret the following quotes by James Allen; Author of As A Man Thinketh

"You are today where your thoughts have brought you; you will be tomorrow where your thoughts take you."

_____

_____

_____

"Man is made or unmade by himself."

_____

_____

_____

"Man is always the master, even in his weaker and most abandoned state."

_____

_____

_____

"Circumstances does not make the man; it reveals him to himself."

_____

_____

_____

"The strength of character gained will be the measure of his true success."

_____

_____

_____

"As he thinks, so is he; as he continues to think, so he remains."

_____

_____

_____

Chapter afterthoughts

What did I get out of this chapter?

_____

_____

_____

_____

How can I apply this chapter to my life?

_____

_____

_____

What will I do differently now?

_____

_____

_____

What questions should have been asked in this chapter?

✂ _____

✂ _____

✂ _____

What can I add to this chapter to make it more powerful, engaging or helpful?

_____

_____

_____

_____

_____

Playing Catch-Up

During your incarceration you will struggle with the past (all the things you did before going to prison), the present (your incarceration) and your future (beyond prison). The past can hold you back if you refuse to let go of it. The present can **stagnate** you if you don't do anything to change. The future can slip away from you because you allowed the past and present to dictate the future. You can't drive a car staring in the rearview mirror. The rearview mirror is for seeing what's behind you, but your main focus is looking straight and seeing where you're going. Take an occasional glimpse in your life's rearview mirror, but keep your eyes focused on the journey ahead of you.

Holding on to the past causes a lot of people to try and play catch-up when they are released from prison. Taking too many trips down memory lane (in your head or during talks with other inmates) has the potential to keep you stuck in the past. Your past has no room in the present or future. Don't spend your time fantasizing about returning to the streets. Leave the past in the past; live in the present preparing for your future.

When individuals leave prison trying to play catch-up on the streets, they think if they go to enough parties, have enough sex, do enough drugs, catch up with all the latest trends and regain their street status, these things will make up for the time spent in prison. Playing catch-up is a failed attempt to fill a void that was created while incarcerated because these individuals did not do anything to improve themselves.

If you leave prison thinking you can *play catch-up* you're setting yourself up for failure. You can't make up for the time spent behind bars. The best thing to do is to make good use of your time while incarcerated, so when you get out you have something positive to show for your time away.

Prison teaches us so many valuable lessons and one those lessons is patience. Leave prison respecting the **concept** of patience and your chances of never returning to prison increase **immensely**. If you didn't have patience before going to prison, you sure know the meaning of patience now; living in an environment where everything is based on controlled movement, that should be enough to teach anyone patience. In prison you have to wait for mail, visits, chow, shower, phone, haircut, an institutional **grievance**, go to rec, leave rec, and so much more. This is the level of patience you have to take home with you. When you exercise patience you can focus better on your direction, and direction is more important than speed because a lot of people are going nowhere fast.

People trying to play catch-up are more focused on getting the things they want, instead of the things they need, so they start off on the wrong foot from day one. Your needs should always be first priority. If you allow your wants to become greater than your needs you will have a problem, because all your choices will be based on the things you want and not necessarily on the things you need. Playing catch-up leads to poor decision making, moving in haste, and burdening oneself with the pressure to acquire materialistic things even if means breaking the law.

Why is *playing catch-up* a pitfall individuals fall victim to when they get out?

_____

_____

_____

Why is *playing catch-up* a trap off?

_____

_____

_____

How can your "wants" jeopardize your freedom?

_____

_____

_____

What happens when your wants become greater than your needs? Explain

_____

_____

_____

Can you "make up for lost time" when you get out? Yes [ ] No [ ] Explain

_____

_____

_____

How does *playing catch-up* put unnecessary pressure on you? Explain.

_____

_____

_____

Why is *playing catch-up* a sign someone has or hasn't changed? Explain.

_____

_____

_____

List some things you *NEED* immediately upon your release.

✂ _____   ✂ _____

✂ _____   ✂ _____

✂ _____   ✂ _____

List some things you *WANT* when you are in the position to acquire them.

✂ _____   ✂ _____

✂ _____   ✂ _____

✂ _____   ✂ _____

Can having your priorities in order help avoid the temptation to play catch-up?

_____

_____

_____

What are some of your priorities while in prison?

_____   _____

_____   _____

_____   _____

What are some of your priorities when you get released?

_____   _____

_____   _____

_____   _____

Chapter afterthoughts

What did I get out of this chapter?

_____

_____

_____

_____

How can I apply this chapter to my life?

_____

_____

_____

What will I do differently now?

_____

_____

_____

What questions should have been asked in this chapter?

✂ _____

✂ _____

✂ _____

What can I add to this chapter to make it more powerful, engaging or helpful?

_____

_____

_____

_____

_____

Attitude Adjustment

When I was a drug dealer I often wondered why I couldn't score a major connection that would help take my drug business to a whole 'nother level. I seen guys who were nowhere as street respected as I handling major weight, but it wasn't until I went to prison I found out why them and not me. After talking to a few guys that knew me or knew of me, it helped me understand why I never excelled in the drug world... It was my attitude. I was arrogant, full of myself, and came across as someone not to be trusted. People respected me, but the people who could help me didn't like how I carried myself so they never presented me with an opportunity to grow. After I digested this valuable piece of insight I vowed to never let my attitude get in the way of being successful ever again.

Your attitude could be the determining factor between your success and potential failure to reach your goals in life. Even if you do the best you can do to make changes in your life, if you do not have the right attitude your efforts will be in **vain**. It's like meeting a pretty woman or handsome man only to learn that she or he has a nasty attitude, such a waste.

Think about your attitude as being your **passport** to a better life, your meal ticket and your business card. Your attitude is one of the most important things that can sink you dead in the water no matter how good the plan you have is. NOBODY wants to deal with someone who has a nasty, poor, bad, negative or crappy attitude if he/she can avoid doing so. Your freedom, relationships (personal and business), and overall future can **hinge** on what kind of attitude you bring to the table.

I used to have a bad attitude problem. I didn't want to hear anything from anybody and I thought I knew everything there was to know. I just knew I had all the answers. My incarceration gave me the opportunity to examine what effects my attitude has had on my life in the past and understand what impact my attitude would have on my future.

A person cannot **embark** on a journey of change without addressing what role their attitude plays in their life. If you already have a great attitude, that's awesome. I haven't met many people in prison who came in with great attitudes. Prison alone can sour a person's attitude.

People who possess a positive or pleasant attitude are usually upbeat and **optimistic**. These are the people who can take a negative and turn it into a positive. Who are not afraid of challenges, and do not give up easily. On the other hand people who possess a negative attitude usually see the worst outcome in a situation, are **pessimistic**, and give up fairly easy.

Believe it or not, changing your attitude can change your life. A good way to access your attitude is to ask close friends or family members to honestly describe your attitude, ask them to give you examples that match their descriptions, and then process that information in a way you can work on changing or improving your attitude. Don't be defiant when you hear answers you don't like, just be honest with yourself and proceed to make positive adjustments to your attitude.

What kind of attitude do you have towards life? Explain

_____

_____

_____

What kind of attitude do you have towards people? Explain

_____

_____

_____

What kind of attitude do you have towards your incarceration? Explain

_____

_____

_____

What kind of attitude do you have towards authority?

_____

_____

_____

Do you feel you need to change your attitude? Explain

_____

_____

_____

Has your attitude ever been a problem for you? Explain

_____

_____

_____

What are 3 things you need to change about your attitude, and why?

1. _____

2. _____

3. _____

Why is important to have a positive attitude?

_____

_____

_____

Why do some people wake up with a bad attitude?

_____

_____

_____

_____

Describe an instance when your attitude has been an asset?

_____

_____

_____

_____

Describe an instance when your attitude has been a liability?

_____

_____

_____

List some things that can trigger a bad attitude?

✂ _____   ✂ _____

✂ _____   ✂ _____

Chapter afterthoughts

What did I get out of this chapter?

_____

_____

_____

_____

How can I apply this chapter to my life?

_____

_____

_____

What will I do differently now?

_____

_____

_____

What questions should have been asked in this chapter?

✂ _____

✂ _____

✂ _____

What can I add to this chapter to make it more powerful, engaging or helpful?

_____

_____

_____

_____

_____

Overcoming Bitterness

Has your incarceration caused you to turn **bitter** and cold towards people and the world itself? Are you disappointed in the people who you thought would be there for you? Bitterness is one of those self-defeating negative energy feelings. Bitterness is un-forgiveness that has **festered** and **fermented** over a period of time. Bitterness happens when we feel someone has done us wrong and we feel powerless to do anything about it. Prison is the ideal environment for bitterness to take root within a person.

During our downward **spiral** of poor choices and reckless behavior on the streets, we always felt we had a few people who would stick by us no matter what we did or what happened. We trusted that some relationships would stand the test of prison, though we knew going to prison was a consequence and often inevitable. We are never truly prepared for that day we have to go. The day we get caught is often on the day we least expected it and 99 percent of the time, getting caught happens in the middle of some chaotic situation we are dealing with.

Once you are arrested, convicted and sent to prison, people you thought would be there for you, either go missing or fade out the picture slowly. The feeling of **abandonment** turns into anger, and anger turns into bitterness. The bitterness is a result of feeling hurt and disappointed. How do you overcome bitterness? How do you move past the hurt and disappointment? How do you heal yourself?

First you have to forgive. Not only forgive those you feel wronged you, but you have to forgive yourself for the wrong you have done to others as well. Forgiveness doesn't mean you have to go around pretending like nothing ever happened or that you have to be friends with the person who wronged you. It doesn't mean you have to forget the hurt either. When you choose to forgive you just give up your desire for revenge against the person who hurt you. Forgiveness is the gift we give ourselves that enables us to stop picking at the scab and start making a plan for healing.

Healing is not a process that can be rushed. There's a difference between getting through something and getting over something. When you *"get through"* something it only means that "something" which caused you hurt and pain has passed, but there's a good chance anger and bitterness were left in it's wake. When you "get over" something, that "something" no longer has a hold over you mentally, physically, or emotionally.

Being bitter sometimes makes us say and/or do things we will later regret. There's a saying that goes, "Hurt people, hurt people." If you're hurting don't allow that hurt to cause you to hurt someone else. When you do that, you just keep the cycle of hurt going and going. When you choose to let go of the bitterness, anger, hate and let forgiveness into your heart, you break the cycle of hurt.

Chained by Bitterness

Don't **dwell** on the past. When we get hurt, we have a tendency to dwell on it. The longer we dwell on the hurt and pain the longer it takes us to heal, **facilitate reconciliation** and rebuild our lives. Bitterness is one of those things that, if you cannot overcome it, will be a ball-and-chain on your life as long as you allow it to be.

Have you ever needed forgiveness? From who and for what?

_____

_____

_____

_____

Have you ever asked someone for forgiveness? How did you ask?

_____

_____

_____

_____

How did asking for forgiveness make you feel?

_____

_____

_____

_____

Why is it hard to ask for forgiveness?

_____

_____

_____

_____

Can you forgive someone who wronged you? Why or why not?

_____

_____

_____

_____

Why should we forgive but not forget?

_____

_____

_____

Is hearing sorry enough to forgive someone?

_____

_____

_____

What happens when you forgive someone?

_____

_____

_____

Name some people you need to forgive

✂ _____   ✂ _____

✂ _____   ✂ _____

✂ _____   ✂ _____

✂ _____   ✂ _____

Name some people you need forgiveness from

✂ _____   ✂ _____

✂ _____   ✂ _____

✂ _____   ✂ _____

✂ _____   ✂ _____

Chapter afterthoughts

What did I get out of this chapter?

_____

_____

_____

_____

How can I apply this chapter to my life?

_____

_____

_____

What will I do differently now?

_____

_____

_____

What questions should have been asked in this chapter?

✂ _____

✂ _____

✂ _____

What can I add to this chapter to make it more powerful, engaging or helpful?

_____

_____

_____

_____

_____

Anger Management

We all know what anger is, because we've all felt it: whether in a heated moment, as a **fleeting** annoyance or as full-fledged rage. Anger is a human emotion. But when anger gets out of control and turns destructive, it can cause problems on your job, in your personal life, and in the overall quality of your life.

If you have anger problems, prison is a place where you can learn how to manage it. If you don't learn how to manage your anger it will cause you more harm then good on two fronts; with your fellow convicts or with the authorities within the prison. Prison shows you how to navigate around the thousands of different personalities in an environment you can't excuse yourself from. Doing time is like walking through a **minefield;** never knowing which mine is live or which is a dud.

There are times you're going to feel angry while incarcerated; angry at the system, angry at the staff, angry at the people around you, angry at the people who abandoned you, and at times angry at yourself for putting yourself in this situation. The challenge you are faced with is, how to not allow anger to take control of you. Anger in prison can cause dangerous situations for obvious reasons.

Everyone has at least one thing that pisses them off, annoys them or just straight makes them angry as all out doors; some people have many things. Those specific things that cause you to get angry are called triggers; triggers are the things that set you off. A very helpful way to manage your anger is identifying what your triggers are. Once you identify what your triggers are, you can recognize each one when they appear thus giving you the warning signal you need to consider your reaction to that specific trigger at that specific moment.

The next time and every time after that, you feel yourself getting pissed off, annoyed or angry, stop for a minute and make a mental note (I encourage you to write it down as well) of that specific things which is causing you to *feel some kinda way, has you in your feelings*, or *taking you out of your character*. You will have identified one of your triggers.

A lot of times people around you know what your triggers are and that's how they are able to manipulate your feelings, and *push your buttons*. Another part of managing your anger is not allowing people to *"push your buttons"*. There are people in all aspects of life whose sole purpose is to find ways to piss other people off, make others mad or manipulate people's feelings. You'll find people like this on your job, in a relationship, in your family, and even strangers. When you allow someone to *"push your buttons"* you give that person control over your feelings. So at any given moment, at that person's leisure, he or she can say or do something that he or she knows will anger you.

You actually have people who will watch you so they can probe your feelings, to learn what angers you and how to anger you, without you even realizing it. People will do little things, subtle things that you may overlook. For example, has someone ever said something to you that pissed you off, and when he or she seen you get getting angry, that person turned around and said, "I was only kidding (what are you getting mad for)?" In that instance that person was probing your feelings.

In a place where feelings are supposed to be suppressed as a survival mechanism, there were guys who thrived off of getting other people "in their feelings" or "outta their character". I used to just sit back and watch the puppet masters at play. For those guys who had anger issues I seen some ugly things as a result of not being able to manage their anger.

Prison is the ultimate learning environment. If you can't learn how to control your anger and other emotions while in prison, when you get back into the world, it's going to be extremely hard to adjust to the lifestyle changes that will keep you out of prison. When you can manage your anger, you exhibit a form or self-control, which can be expanded to other areas of yourself.

Helpful tips to help you manage your anger.

CALM DOWN

- Identify your *Anger Triggers*. Things that make you angry.
- Think before you speak. Don't say things you'll regret.
- Think about the consequences.
- Talk yourself down.
- Walk away.
- Go workout, **brisk** walk or run.
- Talk about what pissed you off, annoyed or angered you in a non-**confrontational** manner.
- Work on finding a solution to resolve the issue at hand.
- Remember getting angry will only make matters worse.

Thinking for other people

Most of my sentence I was housed in maximum and medium security facilties where I was assigned to a two man cell living situation, where I only had to deal with one personality, my celly. When I was transferred to a low security facility where the housing units were set up as dorms (some dorms with as many of 40 to 50 guys) I now had to navigate 50 different personalities in my dorm, at least 500 other personalities on the whole unit, then at least 3,000 total on the whole compound.

Low security was very laid back, more freedom to move around, but the respect prisoners exhibited toward one another was lacking from what you find in the higher security prisons. This was a challenge to me because a lot of the guys in the low never been to a max or medium and a lot of things they did used to piss me off. Instead of confronting guys when I felt they were out of pocket, I just let it go. In life we have the choice to feed into or ignore ignorance and stupidity. I would sit and just observe the goings on; in the tv room, by the microwave, in the laundry room and other places and just tell myself to lay low until it's time to leave this place.

You can't get upset or angry when people do ceratin things because some people don't know the significance behind their own actions. You have to literally think for people to avoid getting angry every-time someone says or does something foolish. You can't meet every slight, instance of rudeness, or perceived diss with confrontation, because someone somewhere will do or say something that you can shake your head at. You're always one bad decision away from losing your freedom or your life.

My "trigger" list. Things that piss me off, annoy or anger me.

1. _____
2. _____
3. _____
4. _____
5. _____

Has your anger ever been an issue for you? If so, how?

_____

_____

_____

What is a sign you are getting angry?

_____

_____

_____

List a few ways to avoid getting angry (not listed in the chapter).

✂ _____   ✂ _____

✂ _____   ✂ _____

✂ _____   ✂ _____

List 5 things you've said or done while angry you now regret.

1. _____
2. _____
3. _____
4. _____
5. _____

Are people responsible for their actions when they are angry? Why/why not?

_____

_____

_____

What are 3 signs someone needs help with "anger management"?

✂ _____

✂ _____

✂ _____

✂ _____

What are some consequences of letting anger get the best of you?

✂ _____

✂ _____

✂ _____

✂ _____

Complete the following sentences

I need to control my anger because _____

_____ .

If I learn how to control my anger I could _____

_____ .

When I feel myself getting angry I need to the following things...

✎ _____

✎ _____

✎ _____

✎ _____

Chapter afterthoughts

What did I get out of this chapter?

_____

_____

_____

_____

How can I apply this chapter to my life?

_____

_____

_____

What will I do differently now?

_____

_____

_____

What questions should have been asked in this chapter?

✄ _____

✄ _____

✄ _____

What can I add to this chapter to make it more powerful, engaging or helpful?

_____

_____

_____

_____

_____

Stress Management

Prison and stress are **synonymous,** they go together hand-in-hand. Everyone will experience some level of stress in his or her lifetime, but not everyone will know how to deal with it. I experienced my fair of stress while in prison and I witnessed the weight of stress crush down on many men like a ton of bricks. I've seen men come fresh off the streets stressin' about girlfriends, family, friends (who weren't even looking out for them), and the length of their sentence. I saw stress break men down until they looked like walking ghosts.

The first rule of "prison stress" management is accepting that you do not have the same power to influence certain situations as you did when you were free. Some people just won't listen or act the same as they did when you were physically present in their life or had the ability to make your presence felt. Stressing over situations you cannot control is futile. Once I accepted the fact I couldn't control the things going on in the outside world, I started putting my energy into the things I did have control over, like my future.

Dealing with the day-to-day **rigors** of prison life; the monotony, the endless routines and the uncertainty about the future, you're going to have some stress filled days, that's the reality of the situation. How you deal with the stress will determine whether the stress makes you stronger or breaks you down. Stress can contribute to stroke, heart disease, and cause you to have a mental breakdown. It can also lead to depression if you don't learn healthy stress coping mechanisms.

In an attempt to escape stress, sometimes people will **indulge** in all sorts of unhealthy behaviors in prison like drugs, sex, and alcohol.

It is essential you develop healthy stress coping mechanisms while in prison, because you will need some of these same mechanisms upon your release. Dealing with daily life events can put anyone on an emotional rollercoaster. Finding a place to live, paying rent, buying food, finding employment, parole/probation obligations and trying to re-acclimate back to society will come with a fair amount of stress. So while you are learning how to deal with stress in prison, you are also learning how to deal with the potential life stresses you will surely face upon your release.

When faced with stressful situations try these healthy stress coping mechanisms. You may use different ones for different situations and sometimes it helps to combine them.

Stress Coping Mechanisms

- Read a good book, magazine or newspaper
- Socialize with friends
- Play cards or board games
- Listen to music
- Take a walk
- Make a list of things you want to do
- Write a letter
- Watch a TV
- Keep a journal
- Take a class
- Stay busy
- Don't let your mind wonder
- Engage in positive conversations
- Talk to people you trust about what's bothering you

It's okay to use short-term **diversions** to **alleviate** stress but you have to develop strong long-term stress coping mechanisms that will help you keep life's stresses to a bare minimum.

What are 5 causes of stress in prison?

1. _____

2. _____

3. _____

4. _____

5. _____

List 5 stresses that come with the criminal and street lifestyle?

1. _____

2. _____

3. _____

4. _____

5. _____

List 5 reasons stress is bad for you?

1. _____

2. _____

3. _____

4. _____

5. _____

List 5 signs you are experiencing stress?

1. _____

2. _____

3. _____

4. _____

5. _____

What are 3 of your healthy stress coping mechanisms?

1. _____

2. _____

3. _____

List 5 potential stresses associated with your release from prison?

1. _____

2. _____

3. _____

4. _____

5. _____

Give some examples of positive self-talk.

✂ _____

✂ _____

✂ _____

✂ _____

✂ _____

✂ _____

Give some examples of negative self-talk.

✎ _____

✎ _____

✎ _____

✎ _____

✎ _____

✎ _____

Chapter afterthoughts

What did I get out of this chapter?

_____

_____

_____

_____

How can I apply this chapter to my life?

_____

_____

_____

What will I do differently now?

_____

_____

_____

What questions should have been asked in this chapter?

✂ _____

✂ _____

✂ _____

What can I add to this chapter to make it more powerful, engaging or helpful?

_____

_____

_____

_____

_____

Changing Your Perspective

"The only thing you sometimes have control over is perspective. You don't have control over your situation. But you have a choice about how you view it." - Chris Pine

When I got to prison my **perspective** on life was very negative. It wasn't until I began to question the **values** and **principles** I had adopted in the streets that I began to slowly change my perspective on my situation, my life and where I fit in the grand scheme of things.

Your **perspective** is the way you see things and your **interpretation** of the things you see. People can have different perspectives on the same topic, issue or situation because we all see things differently. Most times our perspectives are shaped by our experiences and environments, but also shaped by the people who were instrumental in our young learning years; parents, teachers, people we looked up to, admired and respected.

During my incarceration I began to understand I needed to work on the way I perceived being in prison. What helped change my perception about being in prison was when I came up with an **analogy** of my prison experience. *Going to prison can be like dying, your negative actions "killed you" and put you in your "coffin/grave" prison. Buried with you are your negative mindset, your destructive behavior, and your street/prison mentality. The days, months and years you spend in your "coffin/grave" prison, actually become a "womb" which you will be reborn from. Like an unborn child who pulls nutrients from the mother's womb, you can use the knowledge you obtain in the prison "womb" as the nutrients you need to be reborn. When your prison journey is close to being over and you've acquired all the things that you need to live a positive and productive life, the prison "womb" gives birth to the new you.*

Prison literally became a university to me. I wasn't in "prison" doing time anymore I was there learning, acquiring knowledge and becoming wiser. People say, *"experience is the best teacher"* well I planned to walk of out of prison with a PH.D in self-development, personal growth and change. Graduation day would be the day I walked out of prison a free man. I became obsessed with making my prison sentence work for me.

It's hard to put things in perspective when you're going through a tough situation, there's no denying that, but no matter how tough a situation is, you have to recognize that the situation could always have been a lot worse. No matter how bad you think you have it right now, someone somewhere has it worse than you and/or would trade places with you in a heartbeat. You woke up in prison today, but someone somewhere didn't wake up at all.

In order to understand yourself, others, and the world around you, you need the ability to change and adapt your perspective, by looking at a problem from different frames of reference makes the possibilities for solving it easier. Always look at a situation from multiple perspectives and then choose the perspective that allows you a positive outcome.

What is your perspective on doing time?

_____

_____

_____

What is your perspective on life?

_____

_____

_____

What is your perspective on the past?

_____

_____

_____

What is your perspective on the future?

_____

_____

_____

What can make a person change perspectives on a situation, issue or topic?

_____

_____

_____

What 5 things that can influence our perspective?

1. _____

2. _____

3. _____

Is listening to other people's perspective(s) good or bad? And Why?

_____

_____

_____

Has your perspective on friends changed since being in prison? Explain

_____

_____

_____

Has your perspective on the streets changed since being in prison?

_____

_____

_____

Has your perspective changed on "ANYTHING" since being in prison? If so what?

_____

_____

_____

List 3 ways your perspective has changed (not listed) **since using this workbook.**

1. _____

_____

2. _____

_____

3. _____

_____

Chapter afterthoughts

What did I get out of this chapter?

_____

_____

_____

_____

How can I apply this chapter to my life?

_____

_____

_____

What will I do differently now?

_____

_____

_____

What questions should have been asked in this chapter?

✄ _____

✄ _____

✄ _____

What can I add to this chapter to make it even more powerful, engaging or helpful?

_____

_____

_____

_____

_____

Motivation 101

Something or someone motivates much of the things we do in this life. Love, hate, greed, money, revenge, and reward are some of the things that motivate us. When you break motivation down in baby terms, motivation is the force that drives us to do the things we do.

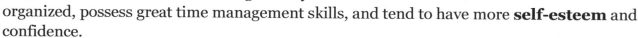

For better or worse, some form of motivation generally guides our actions and behaviors. **Motivation** pushes us to achieve our goals, and improve our overall quality of life.

Anyone interested in personal growth, accomplishing short-term, long term and life-long goals will have to learn how to motivate themselves in prison. People who are self-motivated are generally more organized, possess great time management skills, and tend to have more **self-esteem** and confidence.

Getting motivated and staying motivated is challenging in prison, especially when you're surrounded by a lot of people who have given up on themselves. I remember how draining it was being in the same room with people who never had anything positive to say. But I never allowed myself to let those kinds of people discourage me. I did my best to stay upbeat and optimistic about the future and the things I was doing to shape it.

One of the things that kept me motivated in prison was believing the reality I was living in would not be the sum of my life. I believed with every fiber of my being I would return to society ready to make my mark on the world. I refused to believe that prison was the end of my story. You had to see me operate in prison, you could not tell me I wasn't going to do some great things when I got out.

I created challenges for myself to keep me motivated. Even when I didn't meet the challenge I felt motivation from knowing how much I tried, and the fact I gave it my all. I would learn from where I fell short and go into the next challenge just as encouraged and motivated as the last. The vision I was creating for myself was what ultimately kept me motivated. Old sayings like, *If you can see it, you can be it, If you can believe it, you can achieve it,* or *Nothing comes to a dreamer but sleep,* became my mantras.

There is a strong **correlation** between motivation, personal goals and achievement. In order to get properly motivated it helps to spend some time thinking about your personal goals and what you want to achieve in your life. It is important to remember when thinking about what you would like to achieve in your life, that change is **inevitable**. Once you have thought about your life goals you can start to plan how best to achieve them. Set small goals for the future. In ten years I will be... in five years I will be... etc. Work out plans of action with smaller and smaller sub-goals until you can arrive at an action plan that you can start working on now.

It's tough at times to get and stay motivated in prison, I realized motivation alone wasn't the key to achieving success; I would have to learn how to develop motivational habits.

Motivational habits are the habits that increase your motivation, or drive you even when you're not very motivated. You ever feel more motivated on sunny days then you do on rainy or cloudy days? Why is that? That's because motivation is a feeling, and like any other feeling, motivation will fluctuate depending on a number of factors like weather, relationships, progress, or results. You can't depend on motivation alone to keep you working towards your goals, because there will be days you will feel unmotivated. There will be days you're gonna feel doubtful, feel like giving up, feel like what you're doing is not worth it. When days like that come around (and hopefully they don't last long), the one thing that will push you to continue moving forward will be strong habits, commitment, discipline, determination, internal drive, perseverance, and consistency.

Consistency – Do one goal orientated thing everyday (even if it's for 10 minutes) whether you're feeling motivated or not. Then add another thing, and another, and another, until all those things become a habit. Consistency will build strong habits and strong habits will become part of your daily routine, your daily routine will be part of your lifestyle.

You hit the weight pile on a regular basis because you love working out, but there are days you don't feel like working out (you're feeling unmotivated) because you're just not in the mood, have other things on your mind, or feeling discouraged because you're not the seeing the results you looking for, but you go workout anyway. You workout because working out is now part of your lifestyle and you know if you don't go workout, you'll feel guilty about not going and feel even worse. You also know, once you start working out eventually you'll begin to feel better.

Commitment – Those days you're feeling unmotivated, it's your commitment to accomplish your goals that will drive you. When you commit to doing something, you have to determine that nothing will stop you from reaching your goals NO MATTER WHAT.

Discipline – Train yourself to do the things that move you closer to your goals. Ask yourself, *"if I do or don't this, how does this help or hurt me?"* To accomplish anything in life, you have to develop discipline. You build discipline by recognizing your weaknesses and strengthening your willpower to resist those weaknesses. Discipline gives you the resolve to choose between doing something that is pleasurable but doesn't help move you toward your goals and doing something that is not pleasurable but moves you towards your goals.

Perseverance – There's a quote that says, *"The race is not given to the swiftest or the strong, but those who can endure."* That means you will not give up, quit, or lay down no matter what. That you will stay on this journey of self-improvement, self-discovery, and personal growth until the very end.

Challenge – An effective way to boost your motivation is to set challenges for yourself. Challenge yourself to do things that will help you grow and stop doing things that don't. This tactic will create eagerness and enhance your productiveness. Reward yourself when you meet your challenge and repeat the challenge when you fall short, until your meet your challenge.

What are some things that motivate you in a positive way?

_____   _____

_____   _____

_____   _____

What are some things that motivate you in a negative way?

_____   _____

_____   _____

_____   _____

Explain why everything we do motivated is by something?

_____

_____

_____

_____

What a few factors motivating you to change?

✂ _____

✂ _____

✂ _____

✂ _____

What is motivational fuel?

_____

_____

_____

_____

How can you turn being abandoned by others into motivation?

_____

_____

_____

_____

What are 5 things you can do to motivate yourself?

1. _____

2. _____

3. _____

4. _____

5. _____

List 5 things you can do to motivate others (that are different from the list above).

1. _____

2. _____

3. _____

4. _____

5. _____

You can tell if someone is self-motivated when he/she...

✂ _____

✂ _____

✂ _____

✂ _____

Chapter afterthoughts

What did I get out of this chapter?

_____

_____

_____

_____

How can I apply this chapter to my life?

_____

_____

_____

What will I do differently now?

_____

_____

_____

What questions should have been asked in this chapter?

✂ _____

✂ _____

✂ _____

What can I add to this chapter to make it more powerful, engaging or helpful?

_____

_____

_____

_____

_____

Sacrifice 101

My mom and a few close friends made a lot of sacrifices for me while I was in prison for those 13-plus years, and no amount of money can repay them for that. I learned to appreciate the sacrifices people made for me. Whether it was getting a letter, a money order, or a visit I was grateful for anyone who took the time to check for me. You know like I know, getting a letter can keep you going for a month, a money order two months, and a visit six months or more. I made a promise to show all those who sacrificed for me, I didn't take them or the things they did for me for granted.

Sacrifices people make for you while you're incarcerated

When people do *anything* for you while you're incarcerated, no matter how small that "thing" is, that person is making a **sacrifice** for you. When you get a visit, your visitor is sacrificing his/her time, travel, and visiting expenses. When someone writes you or sends you a package, he/she sacrifices time and postal expenses. The ultimate sacrifice is when someone sends you his or her hard earned money. People make sacrifices for you to show you they care about you, because no one is **obligated** to do anything for you while you are in prison.

It's important to acknowledge the sacrifices others have made and/or are making for you while you are incarcerated. Tell people how deeply you **appreciate** their sacrifices, and how you understand getting a visit, sending a letter, sending money is a sacrifice being made for you.

How can you repay someone who has sacrificed for you during your incarceration? **Monetarily** you can't, but you can repay someone by showing him or her the sacrifices he/she has made for you were not in vain. You do that by changing your game plan and doing something positive with your life once you get out.

Sacrifices you are willing to make to be successful

In order to be successful you have to be willing to give up some things. What sacrifices are you willing to make to be successful? You may have to give up your social life, watching TV, certain friends, and even sleep in order to achieve your goals. One of the most important things you'll have to give up is your old way of thinking. If you want to achieve success in an area of your life, then you'll have to change what you currently believe about yourself especially if your current belief system is holding you back.

Sacrificing for success means giving up temporary comfort to gain permanent success. There can be no success without sacrifice. A lot people say they want to be successful, but not a lot people are willing to make the sacrifices needed to be successful. Success is simple once you accept how much hard work you have to put into it. Success demands **unwavering** commitment. It's the dedication you show on a daily basis towards your desired outcomes that will make all the difference in the end.

Who have made/are making sacrifices for you and how?

1. _____

   _____

2. _____

   _____

3. _____

   _____

How do you plan on repaying those who have sacrificed for you?

_____

_____

_____

What has been the biggest sacrifice you have ever made for yourself?

_____

_____

_____

What has been the biggest sacrifice you have made for someone else?

_____

_____

_____

List some sacrifices you are willing to make to be successful.

✂ _____

✂ _____

✂ _____

✂ _____

Chapter afterthoughts

What did I get out of this chapter?

_____

_____

_____

How can I apply this chapter to my life?

_____

_____

_____

What will I do differently now?

_____

_____

_____

What questions should have been asked in this chapter?

✂ _____

✂ _____

✂ _____

What can I add to this chapter to make it more powerful, engaging or helpful?

_____

_____

_____

_____

_____

Focus 101

Prison has its share of distractions but not nearly as many distractions as there are in society. You can lose focus on the streets so fast, you won't even realize you've lost focus until something happens and you get a wake up call. Make sure you leave prison with your priorities in order because it's real easy to get caught in the *"I'm just getting' home"* **mode**; chasing the opposite sex, looking up old friends, partying and having fun will cause you to lose sight of your goals. A lot of people get too caught up in the **euphoria** of just being out of prison, that they flat-out forget about all the plans and promises they made during their incarceration.

When people leave prison unfocused they think getting out of prison means they are free, and that's where a lot of them go wrong, because if you haven't freed yourself from the mental prison in your mind the simplest distraction has the potential to send you back to the destructive lifestyle that sent you to prison in the first place.

Getting out of prison isn't the challenge, staying out prison is where the challenge lies, and in order to meet that challenge you have to learn how to focus, now.

I knew this guy who always hung out on the weight pile but never worked out, he'd be there talking shhh while all the guys were getting their workout in. One day I asked 'em why didn't he workout as much time as he spent on the weight pile, and his answer was, *"I'm a workout when I get out."* Needless to say I never asked him about working out again. The morale of the story is, DON'T WAIT UNTIL YOU GET OUT TO DO THE THINGS YOU CAN DO NOW, THAT WILL MAKE YOU BETTER NOW. If you can't learn to focus now, while you're incarcerated, trying to get focused in the midst of the challenges you'll be faced with on the outside is going to be extremely difficult.

One of the ways to get focused is by getting rid of the distractions in your life. The things you can't simply get rid of, you have to tune out. The number one distraction you have to rid yourself of is, people who don't **contribute** to your personal growth and positive change. People who are miserable and negative thinking, people who are always the center of some kind of drama, who instigate, gossip, and keep petty squabbles going. These kinds of people are to you what kryptonite was to Superman. You can be focused, doing all the right things and working your plan, but the moment you let people who have no goals or purpose in their life into your circle, you give them the potential to put a monkey wrench in your new game plan.

Distractions can slow you down, stop you in your tracks, or derail your plans altogether. You can usually sense when something or someone has the potential to be a distraction, but we ignore the red flags and warning signals because we always need to feel like we have every situation under control. By the time the distraction turns into a full-blown problem you've already wasted valuable time, **squandered** resources, and possibly let a few opportunities get by you.

I was so focused upon my release from prison it took me 18 months before I found myself in an intimate relationship with a woman. All I did was work and on my free time, I worked on my goals. I was working so hard I had people telling me I needed to take some time out to enjoy myself. The only thing was, most of the people who were telling me to take time to enjoy myself, had been on their jobs as long as I was in prison, were retired and financially stable, so they couldn't understand how serious staying focused was for me. I was on a mission. I'd be lying if I said there weren't times I had to struggle to stay focused on more then one occasion, but each time I found myself a little off course I would evaluate the reasons why, and I would gradually distance myself from that which was distracting me, no matter what or who it was.

It's when everything seems to going good and you begin to see your plans coming together you have to focus even more because you may be tempted to let your guards down. It's in those moments when you let your guards down you become easily distracted and that can cost you; time (wasted on someone/something that wasn't bringing you closer to your goals) or your freedom (when we are not focused we tend to make poor choices and irrational decisions). It's also very easy to lose focus when you begin to doubt yourself or when your goals seem unattainable and you don't see any results for your efforts. This is when you have to double down and focus like never before.

Finish what you start!

If you're like me, constantly thinking and coming up with the "next great idea" it's very important for you to develop a few strategies to keep you focused. It's always great to come up with new ideas, I do it all the time; in the shower, walking down the street, lying in bed and just about everywhere I go I'm thinking of some new project I can develop. The only thing was, I would start projects, but very rarely was I completing them. I got caught up trying to do everything and wound up not getting anything done, so at the end of the year all I had to show for that year was a bunch of unfinished projects.

After I stopped spreading myself so thin, and concentrated my time and efforts on one or two projects at a time I began to see better results and projects being completed. It took me a while to figure out where I was going wrong, but there's a saying that goes, *"Work smarter, not harder."* Start a project, see it through then move on to the next one.

Daily and Weekly to-do list!

Another thing I learned to do was create a weekly and daily to-do list. Along with spreading myself thin, I also found I wasn't being as productive as I knew I should be in spite of working on several projects simultaneously. I knew in my head the tasks I needed to do, but then I'd sit down to do them and be on Facebook, checking emails, looking at YouTube videos and doing everything on the computer other then what I needed to be doing; before I knew it hours would go by and I didn't do anything that was moving me closer to my goals.

A friend suggested I create weekly and daily to-do lists to help me focus on the tasks I should be doing. I tried it and I'm telling you it works. I create my weekly to-do list Sunday evening, and the daily to-do list each evening. When I wake up I can defer to my lists and I get down to business. As the day goes by I'm able to check off the tasks I was able to complete and know the reasons why a task was not completed. My friends, I have experienced leaving prison razor sharp focused, becoming unfocused and having to find my focus again. I can tell you, today, I am as focused as the day I left the penitentiary 10 years ago!

List 3 street distractions and how they can hinder your change/growth

1. _____

2. _____

3. _____

List 3 prison distractions and how they can hinder your change/growth.

1. _____

2. _____

3. _____

What are some ways you can avoid distractions in prison?

✂ _____

✂ _____

✂ _____

What are some ways you can avoid distractions on the streets?

✂ _____

✂ _____

✂ _____

Describe 3 instances when losing your focus can/will cost you.

1. _____

2. _____

3. _____

Compete the following sentences.

People who are focused are usually _____

because _____

People who are focused are usually _____

because _____

Chapter afterthoughts

What did I get out of this chapter?

_____

_____

_____

_____

How can I apply this chapter to my life?

_____

_____

_____

What will I do differently now?

_____

_____

_____

What questions should have been asked in this chapter?

✂ _____

✂ _____

✂ _____

What can I add to this chapter to make it more powerful, engaging or helpful?

_____

_____

_____

_____

_____

A Mother's Pain

Have you ever stopped to think about the impact your street lifestyle and incarceration has had on your mother? I was so caught up in the streets I never took the time to consider how the way I was living was impacting my mother's life. I took my mother through a lot, caused her a lot of hurt and pain. The streets will do that to you; make you selfish and uncaring about other people's feelings.

It wasn't until I went to prison for that long stretch that I was able to **comprehend** what I did to my mother. Through a series of brutally honest talks, letters, and visits with my mother I was able to understand the **depth** of the hurt and pain my brothers and I had caused my mother. She explained how our repeated incarcerations made her feel ashamed, guilty, embarrassed, sad, and helpless. At times my mother said she felt like she failed as a mother. Then there were times she felt angry and alone. My mother had 5 sons and at any given moment one, two, or three of us would be locked up. She talked to me about all those sleepless nights we caused her and how she **dreaded** answering the phone at night for fear of getting that phone call mothers fear the most; the one notifying her that her son or daughter has been killed.

No matter how far we fall, mothers are always there to pick up us up. Through unconditional love and self-sacrifices mothers continue to believe in their child even when that child stops believing in him/herself. Even through all the hurt and pain, mothers very rarely turn their back on their children. My mother said visiting me in prison was hard. She'd be happy to see me during the visit, but sad when leaving. She said it was painful her leaving through one door and me going back inside through another. She said she'd get outside the visiting room and remember something she wanted to tell me and couldn't and how that just broke her heart.

My mother stuck by me day for day from the time I was arrested to the day I was released almost 15 years later. Her belief in me helped restore my belief in myself because by the time I reached prison I was mentally, emotionally, spiritually, and financially broken.

When faced with the decision to change it's always good to do it first and foremost for ourselves, but there's also a list (even if it has one name on it you owe change to. Many times I prayed I'd have a chance to make things right with my mother. I promised God if he watched over her, I'd never take her through the hurt and pain again. I've been with guys who lost their mothers while in prison, and that was something I prayed I wouldn't have to experience while incarcerated. I know a guy whose mother died of a heart attack the day after visiting him in prison. I pray you'll be with your mother again when this journey of yours is over and I pray that you will erase the pain in your mother's heart and replace it with happiness and smiles forevermore. Use this time, this incarceration to get our life together and remember mothers are the main people who sacrifice and support their son or daughter when he or she is in prison.

What are 3 instances you remember making your mother proud?

1. _____

_____

2. _____

_____

3. _____

_____

What are 3 instances you remember disappointing your mother?

1. _____

_____

2. _____

_____

3. _____

_____

What kind of impact is your incarceration having on your mother?

_____

_____

_____

What is unconditional love?

_____

_____

_____

If I _____**I know that would make my mother proud.**

Mom would be proud if I _____.

What are some feelings a mother might experience while her child is in prison?

_____

_____

_____

How does it make you feel to have to see your mother from behind bars?

_____

_____

_____

How do you plan on erasing your mother's pain?

_____

_____

_____

What are 3 things your mother said you wished you had listened to?

1. _____

2. _____

3. _____

To be a better son/daughter I have to....

✂ _____

✂ _____

✂ _____

✂ _____

I never want my mother to (complete sentence below) **ever again!**

✂ _____

✂ _____

✂ _____

Chapter afterthoughts

What did I get out of this chapter?

_____

_____

_____

_____

How can I apply this chapter to my life?

_____

_____

_____

What will I do differently now?

_____

_____

_____

What questions should have been asked in this chapter?

✂ _____

✂ _____

✂ _____

What can I add to this chapter to make it more powerful, engaging or helpful?

_____

_____

_____

_____

_____

40+ Years old & Running Out of Time

Some say you get out prison the same "age" you went in. I saw a lot of older guys in prison who needed to grow up; guys in their late twenties, thirties, and even forties carrying themselves inconsistent with being a grownup. You could tell by their actions and conversations many guys still had that child inside of them who was refusing to grow up. Refusing to grow up is why you see a lot of guys get out of prison and go back to their old ways.

For most people 40 years old is or will be that fork in the road moment when one must decide once and for all to get their life together or not. Like many of you, I had been *free-styling* through most of life, doing what I wanted to do with no regards to the obvious consequences. Free-styling means you go day-to-day without a plan and you spend more time *"going with the flow"* then trying to create a flow of your own. When you're *free-styling* you don't make purposeful goal orientated decisions. You think you can *"get by"* without putting in the necessary work to *"get you by."* I have seen a lot of guys free-styling in prison; still thinking they're on the streets.

With the labor market geared towards younger people, being 40 years old and having a criminal history I knew my challenge to find employment would be a bit more difficult. It's **imperative** that you do all you can do to prepare yourself for the job market now because the older you get, the harder it will become to rebuild your life. Use every opportunity to learn a new trade or marketable skill. All the jobs in prison are the same jobs you'll find on the outside or can lead to entrepreneurial opportunities. If you're assigned to maintenance learn the ins and outs of maintenance work; how to use the buffer, the different cleaning methods and solutions used. Maintenance workers (supers, commercial cleaners make a nice salary on the outside and you can set up your own cleaning service. If you work in food service, you can work in the food industry.

Figuring out your goals and purpose will give your life greater meaning. Your goals and purpose should guide all your decisions, from finding information and resources, to who you associate with, to where you choose to live and how you choose to spend your time. When you create goals and find purpose, you will approach them without thinking about rewards or monetary gain. Your goals and purpose should be the things you would do for free, even if you were getting paid for it.

We live two lives... Life One is your life from the time you're born until the time you reach 35 years old. Life Two starts at age 35 until you die. Life One is your learning years, the years you make mistakes, make poor choices and have experiences you are supposed to learn life lessons from. Life Two is the life you're supposed to live based on the lessons you learned in Life One. You are not supposed to be making the same mistakes, the same poor choices and living your life with reckless-abandonment as you did in Life One, in Life Two. By the time you make it to Life Two you should have had enough experiences, information and insight from Life One, to guide you through Life Two.

Not that I am (before I turn) 40 I want to/need to accomplish?

✂ _____

_____

✂ _____

_____

✂ _____

_____

✂ _____

_____

Why is it hard to rebuild your life after you turn 40 years old?

_____

_____

_____

_____

Have you found your purpose in life yet? Yes [ ] No [ ] Explain

_____

_____

_____

_____

Do you believe everyone has a purpose in life?

_____

_____

_____

_____

Can purpose in life be born out a tragic situation? Yes [ ] No [ ] Explain

_____

_____

_____

_____

If a person is doing the following in prison, he or she is *"free-styling"*.

✂ _____

✂ _____

✂ _____

✂ _____

If a person is doing this on the streets, he or she is *"free-styling"*.

✂ _____

✂ _____

✂ _____

✂ _____

What is some things life has taught me so far?

✂ _____

_____

✂ _____

_____

✂ _____

_____

✂ _____

_____

Chapter afterthoughts

What did I get out of this chapter?

_____

_____

_____

_____

How can I apply this chapter to my life?

_____

_____

_____

What will I do differently now?

_____

_____

_____

What questions should have been asked in this chapter?

✂ _____

✂ _____

✂ _____

What can I add to this chapter to make it more powerful, engaging or helpful?

_____

_____

_____

_____

_____

Overcoming Hopelessness

Living life behind concrete walls, razor wire fences and cold steel can make you feel like you're trapped with your back up against a wall. Prison makes it's hard to see the light at the end of the tunnel when the minutes turn into hours, the hours turn into days, the days turn onto weeks and the weeks turn into months and years. It's easy to lose hope when it feels like the sun doesn't shine anymore and the nights feel bleak. For some, the feeling of **hopelessness** will come and go and for others hopelessness will be a dark cloud hanging over their head every minute of their sentence.

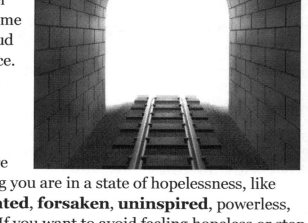

Have you ever wondered why every part of the prison is painted grey? Though there's no scientific evidence, most people associate the color grey with **dreariness**, gloom and doom.

Putting your physical surroundings aside, there are many other factors which can contribute to feeling you are in a state of hopelessness, like being cut off from the outside world or feeling **alienated**, **forsaken**, **uninspired**, powerless, oppressed, limited, depressed, captive, and helpless. If you want to avoid feeling hopeless or stop feeling like you're in a hopeless situation, the first thing you have to understand is, you are not powerless. You have the power to change yourself, thus changing your circumstances. You are your decisions and responsible for everything that happens in your life.

When hopelessness sets in it will make you feel like nothing about your situation will ever change. People get stuck **fixating** on the things that they *can't* change instead of focusing on things that they *can* change. The past has gone and the future isn't here yet, the present affords you the opportunity to change. Visualize, plan, and commit.

I remember those long lonely nights (early in my incarceration awake in my cell feeling hopeless about the situation I was in. All my friends pretty much abandoned me; contact with the outside world was almost nonexistent except for my mom and one or two close friends.

I would lie there still in the night as quietness settled over the tier thinking how far I had fallen and trying to imagine what the future held for me. Sometimes it was hard to imagine getting out of prison a few months before my 41st birthday, after coming to prison at 27. How will I look? Who will be there to greet me when I get out? Where will I go? Who will want me? How will I survive? These were just some of the questions I would ask myself. I would often fall asleep feeling like my life was over. Feeling hopeless.

I would go through the days pretending that doing time was easy, saying things like, *"I can do this bid standin' on my head"* or *"I'm built for this"* or *"next time I'm holdin' court on the streets"*, the whole time frontin'. I often wondered was I the only person walking around the prison feeling like the world had caved in on'em.

I was doing time with people who were doing 5 years to life; some guys even had life plus 10 years, 20 years, and 50 years. There were guys doing multiple life sentences.

112

The thing I found most amazing about this feeling called hopelessness was, most of the guys serving life sentences were the most optimistic and hopeful, yet on the other hand, it was the guys who knew they were getting out one day who were usually overcome with hopelessness.

It took a few years to start feeling hopeful because I was too busy focusing on the negative aspect of my situation. I started to feel less and less hopeless when I realized I in fact had a future, but it was up to me to lay the bricks for the foundation of it. That's when I decided to stop looking for that proverbial light at the end of the tunnel and create my own shine that would light the way through this darkness called prison.!As time went on and the years began to pass my hope was slowly restored as I found ways to keep from feeling hopeless.

The greatest shift from feeling hopeless to hopeful is when I started to believe in myself again. Doubt usually accompanies positive change in the beginning, because you haven't been the person you are striving to be in a looooooong time, so you have to get know yourself again. The more you feel comfortable with the person you're growing into, the more confident you become. Once my confidence was rebuilt my incarceration became a challenge; how can I turn this situation around and leave prison better then I came in, became the ultimate challenge.

Believing in you is the most important tool to overcome hopelessness. Don't just tell yourself you can do something; believe you can do that something. Never say or think, *I can't* always say *I can*. Never say or think, *I think I can* always say or think, *I know I can*. And when other people don't believe you, don't be discouraged, as long as you believe in yourself, your goals, and your vision is all that matters.

When you're going through something it always seems like there will be no end to that "something". Instead of focusing your energy of preparing for the time when the "something" has passed, we get fixated on what we are going through.

My mother used to send me little passages out of the Bible and she would often end her letters, with *"This too shall pass."* As much as I enjoyed reading my mother's letters, it took me a long time to really understand and accept the meaning of *This Too Shall Pass*. But once I "Got It" I realized I had to be prepared when I reached *the light at the end of the tunnel* another one of my mother's favorite things to tell me.

Tips to overcome hopelessness

Think positive
Talk positive
Read positive books
Collect inspirational quotes
Create a plan and goals
Avoid negative people
Believe in yourself
Work on improving yourself

What is hope?

_____

_____

_____

Why is hope important?

_____

_____

_____

If a person loses hope, what happens?

_____

_____

_____

What are 3 signs that a person has lost hope?

1. _____

2. _____

3. _____

What are 3 instances a person can be overcome with hopelessness?

1. _____

2. _____

3. _____

Have you ever experienced feeling hopeless? Explain

_____

_____

_____

Chapter afterthoughts

What did I get out of this chapter?

_____

_____

_____

_____

How can I apply this chapter to my life?

_____

_____

_____

What will I do differently now?

_____

_____

_____

What questions should have been asked in this chapter?

✂ _____

✂ _____

✂ _____

What can I add to this chapter to make it more powerful, engaging or helpful?

_____

_____

_____

_____

_____

Staying Sucker Free

"Stay away from negative people, they have a problem for every solution." - Unknown

A very important part of changin' your game plan is changing the people you surround yourself with. As you begin to change your attitude, perspective, mindset and behaviors you will also have to change the people you associate with. Everybody is not going to be **ecstatic** with your decision to change. Directly or indirectly people will try to discourage and/or sabotage your efforts to better yourself. These are the people we call suckers. Suckers don't support change because they themselves are afraid, resistant and in denial about their own need to change.

There are two kinds of suckers; the ones you can clearly recognize as suckers and the ones you cannot. The recognizable ones are the easiest to steer clear of because they can't help exposing how they feel about you. The reason it's hard to recognize the second kind of sucker is because that sucker will be disguised as a friend or family member. You have to be especially

Sucker Free Life

wary when it comes to the people you call your friends, always remember, todays friend can be tomorrow's enemy.

Frienemies is another word for suckers who pretend to be your friend but are really your enemy in disguise. These type of people are secretly jealous and envious of you and everything you are about. They hate to see you happy or successful.

Suckers have one goal, and that is to get in the way of change, progress, and growth. Suckers will smile in your face and talk about you behind your back. Suckers will take every opportunity to remind you of the negative lifestyle you used to live. Suckers will try their best to convince you change isn't possible.

Staying sucker free is about staying clear of people who bring negative energy, doubt, and disbelief into your space. In prison it's not as easy to simply steer clear of suckers as you can on the outside. Suckers in prison like to stir up chaos and confusion by spreading rumors, gossiping and **instigating** situations. Prison suckers are generally miserable people who are not happy until everyone around them is miserable as well.

Learning how to live sucker free in prison will teach you how to live sucker free on the streets because in prison you are surrounded by potential suckers everywhere you go; in the cell-block, at work detail, the rec yard etc. On the streets you gonna find at least one sucker on your job, in your family, posing as a friend and maybe even **masquerading** as your **significant-other.**

Surround yourself with positive and conscious minded people and don't be surprised when you find yourself growing and feeling good about the future. If you allow a sucker to make you react negatively to a situation that jeopardizes your freedom first, and your progress and growth secondly, you will turn out to be a bigger sucker than the sucker who got you tripped up.

What is a "sucker?"

_____

_____

_____

How can you spot a "sucker"?

_____

_____

_____

Name 5 "suckers" you have to stay clear of when you get out.

1. _____

2. _____

3. _____

4. _____

5. _____

List 3 techniques you use to avoid (sidestep) a sucker.

1. _____

2. _____

3. _____

What are 5 things a "sucker" will say or do to discourage you.

1. _____

2. _____

3. _____

4. _____

5. _____

What is your definition of a friend?

_____

_____

_____

I used to think friendship meant... (Complete statement)

_____

_____

_____

How will you respond to the suckers who try to discourage you?

_____

_____

_____

What are 3 things a real friend would do?

1. _____

_____

2. _____

_____

3. _____

_____

What are other words that describe a sucker?

🖊 _____   🖊 _____

🖊 _____   🖊 _____

🖊 _____   🖊 _____

🖊 _____   🖊 _____

Chapter afterthoughts

What did I get out of this chapter?

_____

_____

_____

_____

How can I apply this chapter to my life?

_____

_____

_____

What will I do differently now?

_____

_____

_____

What questions should have been asked in this chapter?

✂ _____

✂ _____

✂ _____

What can I add to this chapter to make it more powerful, engaging or helpful?

_____

_____

_____

_____

_____

Playing the Blame Game

On your journey of change you are going to stop at places along the way that will test your will and **resolve** to change. Some stops are going to be tougher than others and some stops will make you want to throw this workbook in the trash. Some of the things you'll have to face may not make sense at first, but as you let this new way of seeing life, yourself, and how the world works around you I promise it will all make sense eventually.

Taking **responsibility** is one of those places a lot of people will find it hard to get passed. I was one of those people. In the beginning of my 15-year sentence I blamed anything and everybody I could for my situation. I blamed the system, I blamed my emotionally absent father, I blamed the people who cooperated against me, the judge, the ADA, and I even blamed the guards, yet the only person I refused to blame was myself.

I went through my first five years playing the blame game. It wasn't until I started down the path of change that I had to face a real hard truth, and that hard truth was, I was the person responsible for my incarceration. All the people and circumstances I was blaming for my situation may have had a tiny role in where I was, but it was me who ultimately created the circumstances in which I found myself. Nobody forced me to sell drugs. Selling drugs involved violence. I didn't run and hide from the violence. I didn't have a problem taking the credit when I was making madd money and felt like I was on top of the world, so when the bad times that come with that lifestyle started to happen I really didn't have anyone to blame, but myself. People are very quick to place the blame on others or circumstances in an attempt to **deflect** the role one played in his or her **demise**.

Once I admitted and accepted the truth, that *I was the blame for my situation,* I owned up to that truth and took responsibility for my actions. In that moment, I began to take responsibility for my life; for being in prison, being a bad father, hurting my mother, and helping to destroy my community, as well as for all the other wrongs I had done.

I really don't see how a person can change their game plan, without taking responsibility for his/her past, present and future life. Blaming **external** circumstances for your problems will be a huge obstacle on your journey to improving yourself. There's such a thing as a statute of limitations on the wrongs you feel have happened to you in your life. Once you're old enough to take your life's steering wheel, everything that happens from that point **onward** is your own responsibility.

Playing the blame game will keep you from facing and resolving the issues that have kept you from growing and reaching your full potential in life. Resist the temptation to blame others or circumstance for the events of your life, because each event is the result of choices you have made and are making.

Who is the blame for your present situation and why?

_____

_____

_____

_____

Have you ever played _"The Blame Game"_? Yes [ ] No [ ] Explain

_____

_____

_____

_____

Repeat things someone who's "Playing The Blame Game" would say.

✂ _____

✂ _____

✂ _____

Is "The Blame Game" really about making excuses?

_____

_____

_____

What impact can/will "The Blame Game" have on your life?

_____

_____

_____

_____

Why is it hard for people to take responsibility for their life? Explain

_____

_____

_____

_____

When should you take responsibility for your life? Explain

_____

_____

_____

_____

When you take responsibility for your life, you... (Complete statement)

✂ _____

✂ _____

✂ _____

✂ _____

What are some things people blame for their situations?

_____ _____

_____ _____

_____ _____

People who refuse to take responsibility usually... (Complete statement)

✂ _____

✂ _____

✂ _____

✂ _____

Chapter afterthoughts

What did I get out of this chapter?

_____

_____

_____

_____

How can I apply this chapter to my life?

_____

_____

_____

What will I do differently now?

_____

_____

_____

What questions should have been asked in this chapter?

✂ _____

✂ _____

✂ _____

What can I add to this chapter to make it more powerful, engaging or helpful?

_____

_____

_____

_____

_____

Prison: The Life Saving Factor

There's a prison saying that goes, *"you wasn't arrested, you was rescued"*, which means prison was the intervention a person needed because their life had either hit rock bottom and/or so out of control that death was an **eventuality.** My life was that chaotic. I was so deep in the street life it was only a matter of time before I killed someone or someone killed me; I knew and accepted what seemed like the inevitable. During my late teens to mid-thirties a lot of my friends were either killed or sent to prison for the life we chose to live. For me, it wasn't a matter of if I would meet the same fate, but when I would meet the same **fate**. You know your life is out of control when your own mother prays that you wind up in jail or prison and not dead somewhere on the streets.

In the streets, you're only one split second way from death or a life sentence. Sometimes you get to choose which way a situation unfolds, sometimes it just happens and before you know

it's your life on the line. A simple argument can **escalate** to gunplay. A **perceived** disrespect or slight could be deadly. Drug deal gone wrong, a stickup turns into murder. The scenarios are **infinite**. Every time we stepped foot out the door, there was no guarantee we would make it back safely.

The streets are unforgiving. You can be a rising star, shining star or the neighborhood superstar one minute, hated and **despised** the next. Jealously, envy, and greed turns friend against friend, family against family. Even significant others turn on each other because the streets are a grimy place, filled with cutthroats, **manipulators**, lairs, cheaters, schemers, dreamers, ruthless, and unpredictable people; I became one of them.

Going to prison put me on the sidelines of that life. From the sidelines, I began to see just how dangerous a life I was living. The money, false sense of power, and respect blinded me to the real dangers that lurked around every corner; from the addict who would do anything to get high, the stickup kids, to the dudes who would murder you just because you were out there getting money and they weren't.

Prison not only saved me from the streets, it saved me from myself. I don't even recognize myself when I think of the person I was back then. It saddens me when I think I was ready and willing to kill someone over money and street principles. How many times I came this close to crossing that line. I was a mess, a train wreck waiting to happen in the worst way. On the outside I appeared to have it all under control, but beneath the surfaces the choices I was making were inching me toward deadly consequences. The time I spent in prison gave me an opportunity to find myself, because I was lost. **The streets didn't take a part of my soul, I *gave* the streets a part of my soul, and prison gave me a chance to reclaim it.**

124

In what instance(s) can prison be a lifesaver for someone?

_____

_____

_____

Is prison providing you with a second chance in life? Explain

_____

_____

_____

How many chances should a person get, before society decides he/she has had enough chances? Explain

_____

_____

_____

_____

Should society determine who is changeable and who isn't? Why/why not?

_____

_____

_____

Is prison safer then the streets for some people?

_____

_____

_____

_____

Chapter afterthoughts

What did I get out of this chapter?

_____

_____

_____

_____

How can I apply this chapter to my life?

_____

_____

_____

What will I do differently now?

_____

_____

_____

What questions should have been asked in this chapter?

✂ _____

✂ _____

✂ _____

What can I add to this chapter to make it more powerful, engaging or helpful?

_____

_____

_____

_____

_____

Relationship(s) 101
Building, Maintaining, Repairing

Building, maintaining and repairing relationships will be central to your success during and after your incarceration. Like many of you, I damaged and/or destroyed a lot of relationships before I landed in prison. Some of you are destroying relationships while you're in prison. Time gives you an opportunity to examine your past, present, and future approach to relationships. Whether the relationship is romantic, family/friends, business, job related, or parole/probation based, most relationships are based on a few **core** values; Trust – Honesty - Respect – Communication – Responsibility – **Integrity**.!

In any relationship you have to possess the same values you want the person on the opposite end of the relationship to have in order for the relationship to work. Solid relationships are built over time, not over night. Relationships are an investment. The more you put in, the more you can get back.

Of course the relationship you have with your child or your mother or significant other is going to be different from the relationship you have with an employer or a friend, but the core values remain the same. You want your child to trust, respect, and be honest with you; the same way you want trust, respect, and honesty from others. Healthy relationships give meaning and purpose to our lives and they bring out the best in us.

Building Relationships – start a new relationship with honesty. A relationship that starts with or is built on a lie, will eventually crumble under the weight of that lie. Honesty leads to trust. Trust will not come easily from some people because of your past, so you have to work to earn it. When you treat people with respect, normally respect is given in return. Communication is key to building a new relationship because you want people to be clear, not guess or assume what you are thinking, doing or feeling. In a new relationship you also want people to know you're responsible, dependable, and possess integrity.

Repairing Relationship – When a relationship falls apart it's usually because one or more of the values needed to build and maintain it have been damaged. Trust broken, respect lost, breakdown in communication, and/or loss of integrity are just a few of the reasons relationships fall apart. Not all relationships are repairable depending on the level of damage done. In order to **reconcile** a broken relationship you first have to admit to the acts and behaviors at the root of the damaged relationship. An apology sometimes is not enough. Showing genuine **remorse** for the situation, letting the person who was hurt express his/herself without interruption helps. Talking often helps begin the healing process of a broken relationship. If a relationship is repairable then you have to go back to the beginning and start Relationship Building all over again.

Maintaining Relationships – To maintain a relationship, just continue following the steps in the building phase. **Consistency** will **gauge** the strength of a growing relationship. Are you consistently trustworthy, honest, respectful etc. Build a relationship on the values listed above, exhibiting those same values and the relationship will continue to grow strong.

Why are relationships important?

_____

_____

_____

What is important in a relationship?

_____

_____

_____

Can anyone live or survive without relationships? Explain

_____

_____

_____

_____

What is a strategic relationship? Explain

_____

_____

_____

_____

How do relationships influence our decisions and choices?

_____

_____

_____

_____

What will/can you do to build, maintain or repair a relationship with your....

Children _____

_____

Mother _____

_____

Father _____

_____

Employer _____

_____

Friends _____

_____

What is the quickest way to ruin a relationship?

- _____   - _____

- _____   - _____

- _____   - _____

How do you know when a relationship is over or beyond fixing?

_____

_____

_____

_____

What are some things relationships are built on?

✂ _____   ✂ _____

✂ _____   ✂ _____

✂ _____   ✂ _____

✂ _____   ✂ _____

Chapter afterthoughts

What did I get out of this chapter?

_____

_____

_____

_____

How can I apply this chapter to my life?

_____

_____

_____

What will I do differently now?

_____

_____

_____

What questions should have been asked in this chapter?

✂ _____

✂ _____

✂ _____

What can I add to this chapter to make it more powerful, engaging or helpful?

_____

_____

_____

_____

_____

Healthy Romantic Relationship

Having a healthy romantic relationship can be **beneficial** to your successful transition back to society and achieving your future goals, whereas an unhealthy romantic relationship will be an obstacle and can **potentially** send you back to prison. A healthy relationship involves two people who feel good about themselves individually, care about each other, and are **considerate** of each other's feelings and needs. Like we discussed in Relationships 101, all relationships have some very basic core values that have to exist in order for a relationship to work and be successful. In a healthy romantic relationship you have to add a few other ingredients to make it work.

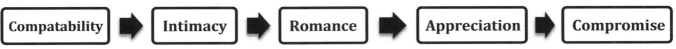

Past bad romantic relationship experiences might leave a person guarded and **jaded** in the beginning of a new romantic relationship so it is important to take your time to get to know someone. Make an effort to get to know each other's likes, dislikes, and opinions. The more you try to know someone, the more you communicate that you are sincere. It takes time and energy to build a romantic relationship; support, motivation, chemistry, love, and happiness. A healthy romantic relationship provides a **nurturing** environment where people can thrive in their life's **endeavors**, on the other hand, an unhealthy romantic relationship is filled with **strife**, stress, sometimes physical, emotional, and verbal abuse. When you are in an unhealthy romantic relationship filled with chaos, confusion, and conflict other parts of your life be affected.

Think of a healthy romantic relationship as a garden, if you maintain the garden, give the garden all the ingredients (listed above) it needs to grow, the garden will flourish and sprout beautiful flowers. If you neglect the garden, abuse it and never give it anything to grow the garden will never grow and eventually die.

Most people have experienced at least one bad romantic relationship in their life; some have experienced a string of bad relationships. To have a healthy romantic relationship you can't bring past emotional baggage into a potential or new romantic relationship. Many people go from relationship to relationship never taking the time to figure out why their relationships keep failing. Before you start a new romantic relationship take time to examine and deal with what went wrong in your past relationships. If you have insecurities, where do they stem from? Trust issues? How did you develop them? Fear of being alone? Did you grow up feeling alone?

Once you can eliminate past emotional baggage you can stop it from being a burden on your new romantic relationship. Explore whether the baggage is your own or was it transferred to you by someone else, like your parents, friends, siblings etc. If you're in a romantic relationship where there's abuse, physical, emotional, or verbal get out immediately. If there's no trust, no respect, no communication, and no honesty my advice to you is to get out of that relationship.

Check what you value in a romantic relationship?

____ Good Looks ____ Religion ____ Personality ____ Patience ____ Understanding

____ Attention ____ Independence ____ Unconditional Love ____ Support ____ Respect

____ Communication ____ Trust ____ Dependency ____ Flexibility ____ Personal Space

____ Intimacy ____ Sex ____ Spontaneity ____ Ambition

What is something you did that ruined a romantic relationships?

_____

_____

_____

_____

What are 3 bad things you have experienced in a romantic relationship?

1. _____

2. _____

3. _____

What kind of "baggage" do some people carry from relationship to relationship?

_____   _____

_____   _____

_____   _____

What changes do you need to make in your life to find and keep a good man/woman?

_____

_____

_____

_____

Give 3 examples of when compromise is good in a romantic relationship.

1. _____

2. _____

3. _____

Is it selfish to ask your significant other to wait for you while you are in prison?

_____

_____

_____

How can a romantic relationship work while one person is in prison?

_____

_____

_____

What do you "bring to the table" in a romantic relationship?

_____

_____

_____

How do you know when someone will make a good romantic partner?

_____

_____

_____

How do you know when someone will make a bad romantic partner?

_____

_____

_____

Chapter afterthoughts

What did I get out of this chapter?

_____

_____

_____

_____

How can I apply this chapter to my life?

_____

_____

_____

What will I do differently now?

_____

_____

_____

What questions should have been asked in this chapter?

✂ _____

✂ _____

✂ _____

What can I add to this chapter to make it more powerful, engaging or helpful?

_____

_____

_____

_____

_____

Prison Parenting

Being a parent from prison is one of the biggest challenges an incarcerated mother or father can face. Add no cooperation from the child's mother or father and it would seem like being a parent from prison is impossible. The steps you are taking to change your game plan will help you become a better parent upon your release. But how do you approach being a better parent now? For those parents who have been missing in action in their children's life even before they were incarcerated, building a relationship with your children will be even more challenging.

Being in prison takes away your **parental** influences, so you won't be able to **exert** authority or discipline your child from prison effectively. As a parent in prison, your role is to become more advisory then **authoritarian**, and when you can learn to accept this, it will make the parent - child relationship work a lot better for you and your child.

As the cause of this situation, you have to be mindful of what your child is going through and not let your own challenges, frustration, and circumstances make the situation about you. Your child is the victim of the decisions you made.

A child might exhibit **resentment** towards you because you're not a constant presence in his/her life, and that resentment might **manifest** itself in rebellious behavior, disrespect and/or anger. You have to be patient with your child and allow him/her to work through any issues he/she has with your absence. Trust is one of the issues that may impact the relationship with your child. The fear of you returning to prison may make your child hesitant to get close to you emotionally. Trust has to be established.

In the process of establishing trust with your child, you cannot lie, tell half-truths or sugarcoat the truth no matter how painful you feel the truth is (to you). If your child finds out that you withheld or put a spin on the truth he or she might never trust anything you say. Be transparent with your child about how you feel, and be willing to answer his or her questions truthfully is a great way to build a long lasting relationship.

In cases where there is no, or limited, communication with your child you can start a letter writing campaign or keep a journal of your thoughts, hopes and dreams for your child. You can then give it to your child when you get out. This is a good way to let your child know that in the midst of your worst life's moments you were thinking about him/her.

Statistically your child will face a lot challenges because he/she has an incarcerated parent. Your experiences, and the poor choices you made can be the biggest **deterrent** to your child potentially going down the wrong road in life. Be prepared and unafraid to answer your child's questions about your incarceration, openly and honestly. Don't be embarrassed or afraid to take a parenting class if available to you, you can learn some things that will help you get back in with your kids and help them understand why you are there.

Tips for Parenting from Prison

Reach out – Establish contact with your child. This may prove difficult depending on the relationship you have with the mother/father prior to your incarceration but it's very necessary. This is where repairing relationships plays a role.

Make a connection - Write and telephone your child regularly. Keep up to date on current events in your child's life. Send cards on birthdays or to mark a **milestone** in your child's life. Learn your child's interests, likes, and dislikes. Learn his/her opinions and perspectives on various topics and issues. Tell your child you love him/her every chance you get.

Listen to your child – Don't assume you know how your child feels or dismiss his/her need to express him or herself. Listen with the purpose of working through issues, the past and/or the relationship you have with their mother/father.

Be transparent – Tell your child how you feel as well, if you feel unsure how to build the relationship say so, but let your child know you will do whatever it takes to build it.

Bad Talk - Avoid talking bad about your child's mother or father. Talking negatively about your child's mother or father could cause your child to feel like he or she is in the middle of whatever issues you have with your child's mother or father. Don't make the issues you have with your child's mother or father, your child's issue.

Incarceration impact on children stats

- 2,250,000 children are estimated to have at least one parent who is incarcerated on any day in America.

- Over 5 million children have had parents who were incarcerated at least once. That is 6% of all American children.

- Over 55,000 American children end up in foster care when their parents are incarcerated.

- Over 50% of current prisoners come from single parent families, or were raised by other family members, or in foster homes.

- 78% of women entering prison are mothers and 64% are fathers. Additionally, 6% of women are pregnant when they enter prison. Most of these women will be separated from their babies shortly after giving birth.

- 50% of incarcerated parents are never visited by their children.

- 85% of prisoners earn less than $25,000 a year before their incarceration, and three out of ten earn less than $10,000 a year.

- In an effort to stay connected to an incarcerated family member, a family may spend almost $250 per month on telephone calls due to the high cost of **mandated** collect phone calls imposed by private phone companies contracted by the prison system.

Source: A Sentence of Their Own - A film by Edgar A. Barens www.asentenceoftheirown.com
- 2010

List 3 ways your incarceration can impact your child?

1. _____

2. _____

3. _____

Why is it hard on a child when he/she has a parent in prison?

_____

_____

_____

_____

What can you do to re-establish a positive relationship with your child while you're in prison?

_____

_____

_____

_____

How can you build your child's trust when you get out of prison?

_____

_____

_____

How can you earn your child's respect when you get out of prison?

✂ _____

✂ _____

✂ _____

✂ _____

What are 3 things you want to teach your children and why?

    1. _____

    2. _____

    3. _____

How will you respond if your child rejects you when you get out of prison?

_____

_____

_____

What happens when a parent breaks a promise to their child?

_____

_____

_____

What does a child want more from their parent, time or money?

_____

_____

_____

How can a bad relationship with the mother/father of your child impact your child?

_____

_____

_____

How can talking bad about your child's mother/father hurt you and your child's relationship?

_____

_____

_____

Chapter afterthoughts

What did I get out of this chapter?

_____

_____

_____

_____

How can I apply this chapter to my life?

_____

_____

_____

What will I do differently now?

_____

_____

_____

What questions should have been asked in this chapter?

✂ _____

✂ _____

✂ _____

What can I add to this chapter to make it more powerful, engaging or helpful?

_____

_____

_____

_____

_____

Overcoming Addictions

Addiction is a condition that results when a person ingests a substance or engages in an activity that can be pleasurable, but the continued use/act of which becomes **compulsive** *and* **interferes** *with ordinary life responsibilities, such as work, relationships, or health.*

Addiction is one of the main reasons people return to prison. People's **inability** to kick illegal substances, old habits, and behaviors tend to lead to poor decision-making, **irrational** thinking and criminal activity to feed their addiction.

Anything you do that becomes *compulsive and interferes with ordinary life responsibilities, such as work, relationships, or health* is an addiction. You can be addicted to drugs (legal and illegal), drug dealing (the money, women, respect, being feared, the excitement, and material **trappings**), and the violence (the feeling of invincibility, power to hurt others). You can be addicted to many other destructive mindsets and behaviors.

Non-substance addictions are more difficult to identify because those addicted normally don't associate their actions and behaviors with an addiction. But the definition of addiction clearly states; *the continued use/act of which becomes compulsive and interferes with ordinary life responsibilities, such as work, relationships, or health.*

It wasn't until I went to prison that I realized I had become addicted to the streets and the lifestyle that went with it. Addiction is the only rational explanation I could find to explain how I lost control of my life. Addiction is funny like that; it will make you think you're in control even you're clearly not. When my life was **steadily** sinking lower and lower into the pit of destruction, I would tell myself, *"You came this far, you can't quit now."* I would also tell myself, *"You've done too much to quit now"* and all I was doing was making excuses for my addiction.

With any addiction, the first step to overcoming it is to admit you have one. If you're in prison doing drugs, selling drugs, gangbanging, stealing, robbing, and being violent you have an addiction. If you are in prison plotting your next criminal adventure, big money scheme, or going back to the same lifestyle that put you in prison in the first place, you have an addiction.

Prison became my rehab. The place I would go cold turkey and detox from all my addiction demons. Being separated from the environment I had become addicted to was a major plus for my need to kick bad habits, a negative mindset, and other bad behaviors, which fueled my addiction.

Overcoming addiction is about looking at all the things that have been damaged, lost or destroyed as a result of your addictions, and making a **vow** to break the habits, behaviors and mindsets that feed your addiction. Prison is the perfect setting to kick the demons of addiction.

Do you have any addictions you need to break? Explain

_____

_____

_____

_____

Can a person be addicted to the streets? Yes [ ] No [ ] Explain

_____

_____

_____

Do drugs dealers have an addiction? Explain?

_____

_____

_____

_____

Can someone be addicted to money? Explain

_____

_____

_____

_____

List other kinds of addictions other than drugs.

- _____   - _____
- _____   - _____
- _____   - _____

What are the consequences of being addicted to the streets or the so-called game?

_____   _____

_____   _____

_____   _____

Are those consequences worth it in the long run? Explain

_____

_____

_____

_____

How do you know when you are addicted to something?

_____

_____

_____

_____

What has your addiction(s) cost you?

_____

_____

_____

_____

What are some "triggers" or "stresses" that can set off addictive cravings?

_____   _____

_____   _____

_____   _____

Chapter afterthoughts

What did I get out of this chapter?

_____

_____

_____

_____

How can I apply this chapter to my life?

_____

_____

_____

What will I do differently now?

_____

_____

_____

What questions should have been asked in this chapter?

✂ _____

✂ _____

✂ _____

What can I add to this chapter to make it more powerful, engaging or helpful?

_____

_____

_____

_____

_____

A Traumatized Life

Most people who have struggled with substance abuse and/or exhibit negative behaviors have suffered some form of trauma in their past. Substance abuse is usually the result of one's attempt to escape the hurt and pain of **traumatic** experiences. Negative and destructive behavior is usually the result of one's inability to understand and/or process the trauma he or she has experienced. There are two kinds of trauma; the kind that happens to you (physically, emotionally, mentally, verbally and sexually), and the kind that happens around you (violence, crime, death, drugs, gangs, gun violence, domestic violence, and sexual abuse). Trauma experienced at a young age, can leave a lasting emotional scar, well into adult years. Some young people have been exposed to and experienced various traumatic situations some adults would have a difficult time dealing with, *as adults*. When you're young, you don't have the ability to process or understand how trauma is impacting your life and influencing your decisions, but if you take the time to explore and confront the trauma now, you might get to the root of your substance abuse and other negative behavioral issues.

During my incarceration I chose to revisit, explore, and confront the trauma I've experienced in my own life in an effort to understand how trauma may have played a role in my decision-making and negative behavior. People can experience trauma and not even realize it. In most instances, as a survival tactic or trauma coping mechanism, we bury the bad things that have happened to us or around us, in the back of our mind.

Examples of traumatic experiences can range from being physically, mentally and verbally abused to seeing a parent physically, mentally or verbally abused. Other forms of trauma included witnessing violence, living in an violent and high crime environment, having a parent in prison, visiting a parent in prison, having a parent on drugs, being raised by a single mother, watching a parent have multiple partners, and the list goes on and on. Everyone does not and will not deal with trauma in the same way. While it may be hard to recognize if one person has experienced trauma in their life, another person might show signs of aggressiveness, anger, anxiety, difficulty focusing, substance abuse, bitterness, hopelessness, stress, being socially **withdrawn,** and distrustful of others.

For each of traumatic event I have experienced in my life; *seeing a friend's mother threaten to jump out a 13 floor window, seeing another friend's mother shot to death by her boyfriend, having two friends die while playing with guns, witnessing fights, stabbings, and shootings in my neighborhood regularly, attending several funerals between the ages of 14 and 18,* there was never any trauma counseling or trauma centers in my neighborhood to access how these events were impacting me. Where I come from, when things happen you are left to deal with the mental and emotional fallout on your own. Looking back, I see how easy it was for me to become a part of the madness happening around me. By the time I was 21, I was entrenched in a vicious cycle of violence, drug dealing, crime, and prison, all of which seemed normal.

The best way to deal with trauma is to find someone you trust to talk to. Whether it's a trusted friend, family member or trauma counselor, talking about the trauma will release you from the hurt, pain, and bad feelings trauma has inflicted on your life, so you can move beyond it.

Give some examples of traumatic experiences that can leave a person mentally and emotionally scarred.

✂ _____

✂ _____

✂ _____

✂ _____

✂ _____

How can trauma impact someone's life?

_____

_____

_____

_____

List things people to do to avoid dealing with trauma (other then substance abuse).

✂ _____   ✂ _____

✂ _____   ✂ _____

✂ _____   ✂ _____

What can you do to stop trauma from being a ball and chain around your life?

✂ _____   ✂ _____

✂ _____   ✂ _____

✂ _____   ✂ _____

What happens if a person doesn't face and/or can't overcome his/her traumatic experiences?

_____

_____

_____

_____

Chapter afterthoughts

What did I get out of this chapter?

_____

_____

_____

_____

How can I apply this chapter to my life?

_____

_____

_____

What will I do differently now?

_____

_____

_____

What questions should have been asked in this chapter?

✂ _____

✂ _____

✂ _____

What can I add to this chapter to make it more powerful, engaging or helpful?

_____

_____

_____

_____

_____

Nothing Sweet 'Bout Prison

I've heard many men call prison *sweet* because the facility they were in had a few **creature comforts** like microwaves, multiple TV rooms, pool table, huge weight pile, central air, late night movies, and chicken/fish twice a week. Prison can **lull** you into a state of complacency if you get too comfortable being there. I never considered prison my home, because I was always mindful what home meant to me. Prison is a manmade environment used to confine those who are serving their prison sentence.

The worst kind of thinking is thinking *prison is sweet*. If you allow yourself to equate incarceration with being *sweet*, you are setting yourself up to possibly come back because you **subconsciously** trained yourself to accept incarceration as a place of comfort. For all the minor conveniences mentioned above, I found many more **profound inconveniences** that served as a constant reminder there was no place like home. Inconveniences that have left a mark on my life till this day.

I hated people having power over me. Telling me what to do, what I couldn't do, when to eat, when to sleep. I hated subjecting my mother to the disrespect some prison staff show our people when they came to visit us. I hated not being treated with a little amount of human **decency**. I hated not getting the proper medical attention when I needed it. I hated seeing brothers die because they didn't get the proper medical attention. I hated having 15 minutes to talk to my loved ones on the phone. I hated prison staff going through my personal belongings. I hated when guys would be ready to kill each other over something dumb. I hated having no rights. I hated feeling my life was in someone else's hands.

I hated eating the same garbage food. I hated prison staff reading my mail, when it came in and as it was going out. I couldn't even seal a letter when I put it the mailbox. I hated seeing my kids growing up in pictures. I hated not being there for my mother when she needed me. I hated not being there for my brother when he was sick. With so many reasons to hate prison, there was no way I was ever gonna put myself back in the same situation again.

Prison is meant to strip you of your dignity and you should not define yourself by the amount of food you have in your locker, the amount of prison currency you possess, or how many pairs of sneakers you own. You should never say things like, *"this is my TV"* or *"this is my phone"* or *"this is my house"*. Don't get attached to anything in prison. The more you get attached to things in prison, the more you become dependent upon those things to get you through your time. I seen so many instances when guys would literary fight or stab each other over the TV, phone or microwave because one or both became so attached to these items they thought they owned them. I've seen guys unplug the phone and dictate who could or couldn't use the phone and for how long. I've seen guys take the cords to the TV or microwave when mad.

I would always laugh to myself how some guys acted like they came to prison with their own TV, microwave or phone. It was so bad in some prisons I've been to, that guys would claim the space they put their chair in the common area or day room; these spaces were called plots.

It's called *"Home Sweet Home"* for a reason, because *"Home"* not only represents a physical place; it represents a state of mind, a feeling, and a thought. Prison is and will never be *sweet*; it's one of the sourest places anyone can find himself or herself.

What can happen if you get too comfortable in prison?

1. _____
2. _____
3. _____
4. _____

Reasons you like prison

- _____
- _____
- _____
- _____
- _____

Reasons you dislike prison.

- _____
- _____
- _____
- _____
- _____

What do you miss most about home?

- _____
- _____
- _____
- _____
- _____

Using one word, what does "home" mean to you?

1. _____
2. _____
3. _____
4. _____
5. _____

Chapter afterthoughts

What did I get out of this chapter?

_____

_____

_____

_____

How can I apply this chapter to my life?

_____

_____

_____

What will I do differently now?

_____

_____

_____

What questions should have been asked in this chapter?

✂ _____

✂ _____

✂ _____

What can I add to this chapter to make it more powerful, engaging or helpful?

_____

_____

_____

_____

_____

Constructive Criticism

Constructive criticism, unlike general criticism, which can be negative, is meant to build you up, not tear you down. Constructive criticism is a useful tool used to promote critical thinking, problem solving and self-improvement. Most successful people know the importance of constructive criticism; it has the power to take you to next level of behavior or achievement.

Criticism is not constructive, and if delivered at the wrong time or at the right time by wrong person (someone you don't respect, like or **deem** worthy), the best intended constructive criticism could be rejected. It's important you learn how to recognize the difference between someone giving you constructive criticism and general criticism (which is unconstructive or has malicious intent).

Some people take constructive criticism too personally, reacting more with emotion than **logic,** and allow what others have said to hurt their self-esteem. These people generally miss the fact that whatever was said was meant with good intent. People become **defensive**, sometimes even verbally attacking the person delivering the criticism. A lot of times false pride prevents a person from entertaining the critiques being delivered to him/her. Accepting any kind of criticism can be a hard pill to swallow, but a healthy dose of constructive criticism can be a good thing if you are trying to grow.

One of the telltale signs of your growth on your journey of change is when you are able to accept constructive criticism, and entertain general **critiques** as well. Another sign of growth is when you don't disregard criticism based on the person delivering the critic and give yourself an opportunity to consider whether the critic has merits or not. *What doesn't apply let it fly!*

It's usually people who care about you who will deliverer constructive criticism. People, who know you the most, want to see you do better, feel you can do better, people who have your best interest at heart; family, friends, teachers, employer and others. Constructive criticism can help improve relationships, thinking and behaviors.

TAKE CRITICISM SERIOUSLY NOT PERSONALLY!

Tips to process constructive criticism:

✂ Recognize the value of constructive criticism
✂ Consider the source
✂ Be open-minded
✂ Admit the truth (even if it hurts)
✂ Don't let false pride put you on the defensive

Sometimes the way we see ourselves is quite different from how others see us. Not that we want to conform to how others view us, we do need our character and behaviors to be consistent with how we see ourselves and with the way we want people to see us. The person who is totally committed to bettering him or herself will not have a problem with people who offer critiques, because he or she will take what can be used positively and roll-out with that, what can't be used positively will be discarded.

Reasons it's so hard to accept any kind of criticism.

✂ _____

✂ _____

✂ _____

✂ _____

✂ _____

What are 5 things you've been criticized for in the past, and by who?

1. _____

   _____

2. _____

   _____

3. _____

   _____

4. _____

   _____

5. _____

   _____

Did you accept the criticisms listed above as constructive or unconstructive? Why?

1. _____

2. _____

3. _____

4. _____

5. _____

How do you determine the difference between constructive criticism and someone hating on you?

_____

_____

_____

_____

Name 3 people you would accept constructive criticism from and why?

1. _____

_____

2. _____

_____

3. _____

_____

What are some honest critiques you would make about yourself? Why?

✂ _____

_____

✂ _____

_____

✂ _____

_____

✂ _____

_____

✂ _____

_____

Chapter afterthoughts

What did I get out of this chapter?

_____

_____

_____

_____

How can I apply this chapter to my life?

_____

_____

_____

What will I do differently now?

_____

_____

_____

What questions should have been asked in this chapter?

✂ _____

✂ _____

✂ _____

What can I add to this chapter to make it more powerful, engaging or helpful?

_____

_____

_____

_____

_____

Fear: The Pros & Cons

Remember that butterflies in the stomach feeling you'd get right before you do something wrong? That's your body's warning signal, that's fear trying to tell you to think about what you're about to do. We learn to push the fear aside, but had we heeded the warnings signals, there's a good chance we would not have done a lot of the wrongs we've done.

Fear can work for you and fear can work against you. Most people never associate fear with being a good thing, but if you learn how to process fear, you can turn certain fears into an asset.

The Pros of Fear – Fear is a positive thing when you learn to be fearful of the consequences of your actions. When you fear the consequences of your actions there's a greater chance fear will keep you mindful of your choices, decisions, and behaviors when there is a risk of losing something important to you, like your life, freedom, job or relationship. Fear of consequences can become a powerful trigger that makes you stop and think before making a decision that can have negative results.

The fear of losing something can keep your **tendency** to make a poor choice, bad decision, or negative impulsive behavior in check. The fear of returning to prison can be a strong deterrent to participating in behaviors that can **jeopardize** your freedom. In instances like these, fear is a good thing.

The Cons of Fear – The street culture teaches us not to be fearful of anything; violence, prison, and death. But as soon as you eliminate the fear factor, you eliminate the lines one normally wouldn't cross because he/she fears the consequences of his/her actions. When the lack of fear causes you to indulge in behaviors that jeopardize your freedom and/or life, living without fear is a negative.

Fear is also a negative thing when it stops you from changing, moving forward, or trying something new. In this **instance** fear works against you. You have to identify what you're afraid of, examine the root cause of the fears, and once you know the cause you are better equipped to face and overcome them.

Fear that **stems** from childhood or family **trauma**, as well as bad experiences makes us play safe when we're up against a challenge. We build a wall around ourselves, which shield us from the feeling of embarrassment, being hurt, facing rejection, or possible failure.

It's good to talk about your fears with people you trust. Not talking about your fears is like hiding them in the closest, you know they are there, but as long as you don't have to see them you don't have to deal with them. Think about what you have to gain by overcoming your fear; you get to move on to the next chapter of your life free of the fears that have been holding you back.

Admitting we fear something does not make us weak, it actually makes us strong because we can be ourselves and unafraid of how other people receive us. We no longer have to hide behind these unwritten rules and codes of street conduct when we learn how fear can be an asset or liability to our life.

Does admitting you fear something make you weak?

_____

_____

_____

What are 3 fears you have that can/will work in your favor upon release?

1. _____

2. _____

3. _____

What are 3 fears you have that work against you?

1. _____

2. _____

3. _____

What are 3 things you fear losing the most and why?

1. _____

_____

2. _____

_____

3. _____

_____

What some fears you've faced and overcome in your life?

• _____

• _____

• _____

• _____

Do you have a fear of returning to prison?

_____

_____

_____

Do you fear growing old in prison?

_____

_____

_____

Do you fear the stigma of having been to prison carries?

_____

_____

_____

Do you fear people will not be supportive when you get out? Why/why not?

_____

_____

_____

List some fears people might have about getting out of prison.

- _____
- _____
- _____
- _____
- _____
- _____
- _____

Chapter afterthoughts

What did I get out of this chapter?

_____

_____

_____

_____

How can I apply this chapter to my life?

_____

_____

_____

What will I do differently now?

_____

_____

_____

What questions should have been asked in this chapter?

✂ _____

✂ _____

✂ _____

What can I add to this chapter to make it more powerful, engaging or helpful?

_____

_____

_____

_____

_____

Reversing the Hustle

Most people associate the word *hustle* with negativity, but a hustle or your hustle is the method you use to earn and/or **generate** income. A hustle can be a 9 to 5 or the thing that earns you extra income.

Contrary to popular belief there's no such thing as a natural born hustler. People learn how to hustle and just like anything else, some people are average, above average, extraordinary at it. Average hustlers will put in the minimum amount of work and effort into their hustle and are satisfied with having just enough. Above average hustlers will put more work into the hustle then an average hustler, but will become content once he or she reaches a certain level of success. An extraordinary hustler will spend every waking moment dedicated to his or hustle in one shape, form, or fashion. The extraordinary hustler's choices are dictated by his or her hustle and he or she eat sleeps and breathe the hustle.

Whatever the level of the hustler, they usually have one thing in common though; they each possess an entrepreneurial spirit. Hustlers can recognize and capitalize on opportunity when others can't. Those hustlers who excel in their entrepreneurial endeavors are willing to put in the necessary work and make the necessary sacrifices to achieve the ultimate level of success. Hustlers don't wait for things to happen; instead they go out and make things happen.

Every hustler knows the hustle comes with a certain amount of risk. If you hustle illegally, you run the risk of losing your freedom or your life. If you hustle as an entrepreneur, you run the risk of losing the money and time you invested in your endeavor. Even if your hustle is a "9 to 5" you run the risk of losing your job for any number of reasons regardless of how much time you put in on the job.

A lot more work and energy goes into hustling illegally, than goes into a legal hustle because there's a lot more factors involved. Trying to avoid detection by law enforcement, stickup kids, rivals, and jealous sideliners go with the illegal hustle. Being available 24 hours a day, 7 days a week to your customers is another factor. Imagine if you used all the time and energy you invested in your illegal hustle and redirected it into a legal hustle, think how successful you could be. Imagine all the potential rewards you could gain from your legal hustle versus all the potential loses you will be faced with from an illegal hustle.

Reversing the hustle is just redirecting your energy and using your transferable street skills for a positive endeavor, whether it's a job, being an entrepreneur, or opening up a small business. To be a true hustler you also have to have a hustler's mentality. A hustler's mentality is taking an *"I'm a make it happen, regardless what it takes"* approach to your hustle. Looking at the hustle from a positive perspective, the same motto still stands but with an added twist, *"I'm a make it happen regardless what it takes, as long as it doesn't jeopardize my life, freedom, or love ones."*

Successful hustlers know talk is cheap and time is a very expensive commodity. You're not going to catch an extraordinary hustler "lipperfessing" about the things he/she wants to do because he or she will be too busy *doing*. **Don't talk about your hustle, be about your hustle.**

List hustles you had as a kid.

✂ _____

✂ _____

✂ _____

✂ _____

List hustles you had as an adult.

✂ _____

✂ _____

✂ _____

✂ _____

Can you flip any of those hustles listed above into a legal hustle?

_____

_____

_____

What are the work ethics of a hustler?

_____

_____

_____

Name an Average, Above Average and Extraordinary Hustler.

_____ is an average hustler because _____

_____

_____ is an above average hustler because _____

_____

_____ is an extraordinary hustler because _____

_____

List things a drug dealer and a legitimate businessman need to possess to run a successful business? *Ex: Keep track of inventory*

✎ _____   ✎ _____

✎ _____   ✎ _____

✎ _____   ✎ _____

List skillsets you can transfer from your street hustle to your legal hustle. *Ex: Pay attention to details*

✎ _____   ✎ _____

✎ _____   ✎ _____

✎ _____   ✎ _____

List the sacrifices you are willing to make for your hustle?

✎ _____   ✎ _____

✎ _____   ✎ _____

✎ _____   ✎ _____

What are some jailhouse hustle/jobs that can be asset when you get out?

✎ _____   ✎ _____

✎ _____   ✎ _____

✎ _____   ✎ _____

How much and what kind of energy goes into committing crime? Explain

_____

_____

_____

List 3 things all hustlers should know? Explain

1. _____

_____

2. _____

_____

3. _____

_____

What are some consequences of an illegal hustle? Explain

_____

_____

_____

What are some benefits of a legal hustles?

_____

_____

_____

How much time should you dedicate to your hustle? Explain

_____

_____

_____

What 3 things make the difference between an ok, good and extraordinary hustler? Explain

1. _____

_____

2. _____

_____

3. _____

_____

Chapter afterthoughts

What did I get out of this chapter?

_____

_____

_____

_____

How can I apply this chapter to my life?

_____

_____

_____

What will I do differently now?

_____

_____

_____

What questions should have been asked in this chapter?

✂ _____

✂ _____

✂ _____

What can I add to this chapter to make it more powerful, engaging or helpful?

_____

_____

_____

_____

_____

Learning to Appreciate

Sometimes we have to lose everything to **appreciate** anything. Being incarcerated is a cold **sober** reminder of how much we take for granted in this life. We choose a lifestyle that falsely promises everything but leaves us with nothing in return. With tomorrow not being promised to anyone, we live a life that takes so much for granted; freedom, family, love, time, and more. Prison taught me to have a **newfound** appreciation for every aspect of my life, no matter how small. From the simplest things like going to bed when I want or calling someone on the phone, to the most profound moments that bring me joy, I take the time to appreciate all the wonders life has to offer.

Finding something to be appreciative of in a bad situation can seem like looking for a needle in a haystack. In spite of where we are, or what we are be doing, there's always something in our life worthy of appreciation. No matter how bad things are in your life right now, things could have always been a lot worse. It can be difficult to appreciate what we have in life because we're always too busy looking at and longing for the things we don't have. We get sidetracked by, or get stuck in the wanting, needing, and not having, instead of the being thankful.

You've heard stories of people waking up in the hospital after having a near death experience and changing their whole life around for the better. Well I haven't had a near death experience but from the stories I've heard and read, I could say my prison experience gave me the same newfound appreciation for life as those who have almost died. When I first got to prison, I used to feel like I was dead in a sense; dead to the outside world at least.

Losing so many people close to me to the streets, AIDS, and the penitentiary I learned how to count my blessing after a few years. I began to be thankful I was doing 15-years, because I could have been doing life like so many men around me, or I could be dead like a lot of my friends. Every night we close our eyes to sleep there's no guarantee we will open them again in the morning, so every morning you do get to open your eyes be thankful, feel blessed, and appreciate the things your eyes will see that day.

You always hear people say, "you need to count your blessings" but how many people actually stop to count their blessings? Well I challenge to literally sit down with a pen and paper and count all your blessings; things you are appreciative for having no matter how small or insignificant you might think that thing is. As your list begins to grow you will be quite surprised by how much you have to appreciate.

For some people, prison is a blessing in disguise. Only the individual can determine that, but had it not been for prison a lot of people would have checked out a looooooong time ago. If you feel you have nothing to be appreciative of, appreciate the fact that you are still here (alive), that's a good place to start. As long as you're alive you have a chance to change and be a better person.

Appreciate the process of change and the journey to self-discovery you are on. Appreciate the time you spend working on yourself, getting to know and learning things about yourself.

What have you taken for granted in the past?

✎ _____   ✎ _____

✎ _____   ✎ _____

✎ _____   ✎ _____

Who have you taken for granted in the past?

✎ _____   ✎ _____

✎ _____   ✎ _____

✎ _____   ✎ _____

What do you appreciate now more than ever?

✎ _____   ✎ _____

✎ _____   ✎ _____

✎ _____   ✎ _____

Who do you appreciate now more than ever?

✎ _____   ✎ _____

✎ _____   ✎ _____

✎ _____   ✎ _____

What has your incarceration taught you about appreciation?

_____

_____

_____

How will you show your appreciation in the future?

_____

_____

_____

I appreciate my......   (Complete each sentence and be creative)

parents because _____

family because _____

friends because _____

eyesight because _____

heart because _____

mind because _____

good health because _____

tears because _____

disappointments because _____

fears because _____

pain because _____

sadness _____

happiness because _____

enemies because _____

time because _____

music because _____

mistakes because _____

I appreciate......

a sunset because _____

the moon and stars because _____

the air I breathe because _____

kind strangers because _____

heartbreaks because _____

laughter because _____

love because _____

life's challenges because _____

life because _____

a good laugh because _____

a good cry because _____

honesty because _____

a hot shower because _____

a kind word because _____

trustworthy people because _____

people who appreciate me because _____

myself because _____

Chapter afterthoughts

What did I get out of this chapter?

_____

_____

_____

_____

How can I apply this chapter to my life?

_____

_____

_____

What will I do differently now?

_____

_____

_____

What questions should have been asked in this chapter?

✂ _____

✂ _____

✂ _____

What can I add to this chapter to make it more powerful, engaging or helpful?

_____

_____

_____

_____

Your Presentation Game

You've worked on your attitude, managing your anger, overcame bitterness, stopped playing the blame game, and you're finally taking responsibility for your life. Wow, you've come a long way. You've addressed your **shortcomings**, faced your fears, strengthened your weaknesses, and everyday you're mentally preparing for your release, now it's time to work on your **presentation** game.

You've worked hard on your **internal** makeover, now it's time to work just as hard on your external makeover. In most cases we only have one chance to make a first impression so it's important to make that first impression a long lasting one.

Your presentation game **consists** of appearance, **mannerism,** and how well you **articulate** yourself. These three things are like the icing on the cake of your change. Your presentation game has the ability to open doors, which normally may have been closed to you for various reasons, as well as keep you locked out of such spaces because of poor presentation.

Your success and livelihood can very well depend on how good your presentation game is. It takes time and practice to sharpen your presentation skills. First, you have to visualize how you want the world to see you, and then you have to actively work towards being able to project that image. ***If you can see it, you can be it.*** Start by **upping** your vocabulary, reading biographies of successful people, and practice speaking without so much street **verbiage**.

Practice your speaking skills on the prison guards and staff until you have your flow down-packed. Then begin practicing your speaking skills on your family and close friends. Don't be afraid how they might react, just tell them the truth; you're trying to learn how to speak so people who don't come from the streets can understand you. You don't have to know or use big words; you just have to be able to communicate clearly. How you speak around your friends is one thing, how you talk to an employer, professionals and people who don't come from or share your experiences is another thing.

I come from the streets and been to prison, but you would never know it unless I told you, because I know how to flip my flow to fit the environment I'm navigating through. This is the part where you have to understand you can't take the streets everywhere you go in life. Present yourself, as you want the world to see you, because the way you present yourself is your life's business card.

In this fast paced world your presentation game is what you're going to use to sell yourself. Carry yourself with confidence. Learn how to talk about your strengths, skills ,and values without sounding cocky. Don't pretend to know about things you don't, stay in your lane. Be yourself. Talk passionately when discussing your goals, plans, and why you can be an asset.

What does your appearance say about you now?

_____

_____

_____

3 places, times or situations not appropriate to use street language? Why?

1. _____

_____

2. _____

_____

3. _____

_____

Is it wrong for people to judge you on your appearance? Explain

_____

_____

_____

What is appropriate attire for a job interview or business meeting? Explain

_____

_____

_____

List some street words or terms you shouldn't use on a job interview or business meeting?

✂ _____   ✂ _____

✂ _____   ✂ _____

✂ _____   ✂ _____

✂ _____   ✂ _____

What do you think about people who speak proper English?

_____

_____

_____

How does mainly speaking street language hinder you?

_____

_____

_____

What does "selling yourself," mean?

_____

_____

_____

What are 3 scenarios you might have to "sell yourself" in?

1. _____

2. _____

3. _____

Name 3 people who have powerful presentation games and why you think so.

1. _____

_____

2. _____

_____

3. _____

_____

4. _____

_____

Chapter afterthoughts

What did I get out of this chapter?

_____

_____

_____

_____

How can I apply this chapter to my life?

_____

_____

_____

What will I do differently now?

_____

_____

_____

What questions should have been asked in this chapter?

✂ _____

✂ _____

✂ _____

What can I add to this chapter to make it more powerful, engaging or helpful?

_____

_____

_____

_____

_____

Values and Principles

Values are principles or beliefs people hold about things that are important to them and reflect what one thinks is right or wrong in any given situation. Your character, from the things you say to the way you behave, should match your values.

There are two types of values systems, a negative one and a positive one. The values that were **instilled** in you as a kid are normally part of the positive value system, and the values you learned in the streets/prison are normally part of the negative value system. The streets and prison have their own set of values, principles, and codes that are sometimes disguised as positive values but run counter to the positive value system.

Normally one's values are rooted in the way he/she was raised; taking value and principles **cues** from people close to them as they grew up. During the learning stage, the importance of values could get **distorted** if you witnessed people you looked up to, to teach you values, not practice the same values they were trying to instill in you.

Examining what kinds of values you have can help you evaluate your actions, decisions,

and the rationale you might use to justify your behavior. An honest examination of your values will determine if your values are realistically in line with your actions. Your values (should) determine your priorities and influence all your decisions; your friends, goals, relationships, and how you spend your time.

Your values are a core part of who you are and who you want to be. Identifying and understanding your values can act as a guide to help you make better choices in any situation.

On the streets and in prison we live by a set of self-serving values and principles, which we use to justify or rationalize our negative behavior. A set of values and principles so poisonous, we are willing to beat, stab, and kill one another over petty principles.
We say we value family, but we engage in behavior that takes us away from family. We commit crime to *"feed our kids"* but the crimes we commit have nothing to do with food.

The set of values and principles we live by on the streets/prison are for survival purposes. If you don't move according to these very often-strict codes of conduct, your reputation, street earnings, and life could very well be at stake, so for self-serving purposes we are willing to put our positive values aside and adhere to the negative value system that dictates life on the streets and in prison. Even in the **midst** of living a dishonest life, people pretend to live by a set of positive and honest values. That's why you'll see a drug dealer going to church every Sunday or giving out turkeys on Thanksgiving, but deep-down under the surface you'll still find that grimy, dishonest, (potentially) violent, scheming, ruthless, addicted to money, and power hungry individual.

Now that you're choosing a new path for your life, you have to decide what matters to you the most; *family, freedom, hard work, honesty, righteousness, peace, life, love, happiness, friendship, integrity, etc.,* and commit yourself to live by those values which are in line with what matter to you most.

Every man and woman should have values and principles, but it's the type of values and principles he/she has that will tell the true character of the person. Ask yourself is the street and prison value system something you want to pass down to your sons and daughters or grandchildren? I'm pretty sure the answer will be no because you know the truth about this system of street/prison values and principles.

We can no longer live by a set of values and principles we are willing to kill each other over or spend the rest of life in prison because of. We put too much value on materialistic living. We value how we look over how we live. In the streets it's all about the image of success as opposed to being successful. We have to get away from this phony value system we've fallen victim to. It's time we go back to that original set of values that were instilled in us early on in life, and for those who might not have that early foundation to fall back on, it's time to learn a positive set of values that will guide you positively.

Adopting New Values and Principles

The worst of situations can bring out the best in people. Prison positives are the positive life lessons you can **extract** from your incarceration that can shape, mold, and guide your life in a new positive direction. Your prison experiences can put you back in touch with the positive values and principles that were instilled in you long ago, or teach you a set of new positive values to base your life on.

As you build your list of positive values in **accordance** to what's important to you, at the same time you'll be building certain character traits that are important on the outside. Positive values and principles can show a person how to project strong moral character successfully.

How does one adopt new values and principles after believing in a negative value system for so long? Easy. Make a list of all your current values and principles, examine them, and then make a list of the benefits as well as the consequences of these values and principles.

Make a list of people who may share your values and principles (and if most the people you come up with are criminals, whether **fictional** or real, living or dead, that will speak for itself). Make a list of the people who tried to instill positive values and principles in you when you were young; your mother, grandmother, aunt, uncle, a teacher, etc. Then analyze which values and principles worked for you and which worked against you. Then you'll figure out which values and principles you'll want to retain and which ones you need to drop like a bad habit.

Doing this is almost like **rebooting** your value system to work positively again. Your core set of values have been there the whole time, you just chose to push them aside because the negative street values were self-serving and more rewarding (so you thought) to you at the time.

For those people who didn't receive any guidance in positive values and principles during childhood, accepting the basic concept of what's right and what's wrong is where you can begin to build a positive value system. This workbook is another great tool for you to use as you build the foundation for your value system.

List the kinds of positive values and principles a person should posses?

✂ _____   ✂ _____

✂ _____   ✂ _____

✂ _____   ✂ _____

Name people who had greatest influence (Positively or Negatively) **on your values and principles as a child and what did they teach you?**

✂ _____

✂ _____

✂ _____

✂ _____

✂ _____

What kind of values and principles do I have and/or follow?
Ex: Do I have Integrity? Am I honest? Am I trustworthy? Am I grimy?

_____

_____

_____

Are my values and principles based on a negative or positive mindset? Explain

_____

_____

_____

Why is having integrity important?

_____

_____

_____

What kinds of values and principles do I need to adopt and/or change to become a better person?

_____   _____

_____   _____

_____   _____

List 3 consequences of having negative values and principles.

1. _____

2. _____

3. _____

List 3 benefits of having positive values and principles.

1. _____

2. _____

3. _____

List 3 people who share the kinds of values and principles with you?

1. _____

2. _____

3. _____

3 instances you will be judged on your values and principles?

1. _____

2. _____

3. _____

How can a reputation for keeping your word help you be successful?

_____

_____

_____

Chapter afterthoughts

What did I get out of this chapter?

_____

_____

_____

_____

How can I apply this chapter to my life?

_____

_____

_____

What will I do differently now?

_____

_____

_____

What questions should have been asked in this chapter?

✂ _____

✂ _____

✂ _____

What can I add to this chapter to make it more powerful, engaging or helpful?

_____

_____

_____

_____

_____

Pride: The Pros and Cons

Pride is a feeling like love. There's different kinds of love, like there's different kinds of pride. Being proud of yourself and your work is one kind of pride. Seeing yourself as better than other people is another pride. The first one is good and the other one is bad.

The Pros of Pride - Pride is necessary for successful **progression**. Being proud of yourself is a healthy feeling, but must be **sustained** by positive future actions. When you're proud of yourself, work, and achievements you become more confident and will want to work even harder to become even better. The pride you feel from reaching a goal makes you feel like anything is possible and will motivate you to embark on the next endeavor.

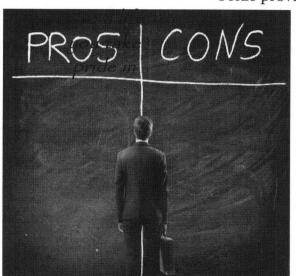

Pride provides you with a feeling of satisfaction **derived** from your accomplishments. Pride helps boost our self-esteem. Pride as an emotion, is a positive character **trait** that drives and inspires us to do well in whatever we pursue. It is an attitude, which separates excellence from **mediocrity**.

Pride can create a high work **ethic** as well as place importance on education, work, family, and other aspects of a person's life. Taking pride in your work says a lot about your overall character. When a person has a sense of pride, he/she has a better attitude, gets better results and is someone others want to be like. Pride gives you a sense of your own value or worth as a person and it shows how much you like, accept, approve, and respect yourself.

The Cons of Pride- Pride is not **inherently** bad, possessing too much pride can be overpowering and cloud one's judgment. People with too much pride are **boastful**, have an **unrealistically** high opinion of themself, and think they are better than everyone else. Being too prideful causes a person to be so concerned about his/her public image it creates a hardship on him/her. So worried about what others will think, a person with too much pride will refuse to work in a fast food restaurant or take a minimum wage job, even though he/she has no other means of income.

Being overly prideful can prevent you from doing what you know is right. It can keep you from asking for help. It can block **empathy** and make you seem cold and uncaring. It can keep you from happiness because pride is a hard substitute for love. Sometimes pride can hinder you from growing as a person and it can cause you to lose some good people and things in your life.

In certain instances, it's ok to put your pride aside if it helps you get closer to your goals, so if you have to work that minimum wage job or live frugally for a while, it's ok because what you're doing is a means to an end. Don't allow foolish pride get in the way of the bigger picture. We do what we have to do now, so we can do what we want to do later.

What do you take pride in?

_____   _____

_____   _____

_____   _____

_____   _____

What are 3 advantages of having pride?

1. _____

2. _____

3. _____

What are 3 disadvantages of having too much pride?

1. _____

2. _____

3. _____

What are 3 instances you let pride get in the way and what did it cost you?

1. _____

   _____

2. _____

   _____

3. _____

   _____

How can pride boost your self-esteem?

_____

_____

_____

How can too much pride get in the way of your success?

_____

_____

_____

What can you do to stop pride from getting the best of you?

_____

_____

_____

Others might confuse your pride with?

_____

_____

_____

A person who takes pride in him/herself is more likely to?

_____

_____

_____

What are instances its okay to put our pride aside?

✂ _____

✂ _____

✂ _____

What is misguided pride, and how can it get in the way of your success?

_____

_____

_____

Chapter afterthoughts

What did I get out of this chapter?

_____

_____

_____

_____

How can I apply this chapter to my life?

_____

_____

_____

What will I do differently now?

_____

_____

_____

What questions should have been asked in this chapter?

✀ _____

✀ _____

✀ _____

What can I add to this chapter to make it more powerful, engaging or helpful?

_____

_____

_____

_____

People, Places & Things

People, places, and things can either keep you out of prison or send you back. This is the simplest, yet one of the most powerful concepts a person getting out of prison needs to have **embedded** in their brain as he or she prepares for their release. If you keep this concept in the forefront of your mind you'll find it extremely helpful as you settle into your new life after prison. Some of the people you used to hangout with you have to stay away from now. A lot of the places you used to go you can't go any more, and a lot of things you used to do you can't do anymore if you are serious about making changes in your life.

People – The people you surround yourself with, or just associate with can have a negative or positive impact on your quest to stay out of prison. A simple association with someone who is involved illegal or negative behaviors can **jeopardize** your freedom and/or your life. It's unfortunate but you have to keep your distance from anyone who is not living a positive and law-abiding life. You know the terms, *"Birds of a feather flock together", "Guilty by association", "Show me your friends, and I'll tell you who you are."* You get caught-up in a situation with the wrong people, right or wrong, your criminal history can sink you. Surrounding yourself with positive people and your chances of finding yourself in negative situations decreases. Negative people attract negative situations.

Places – There's a general rule about places; if you hangout, frequent, or find yourself in places where there's a possibility of violence, drug activity, or feel you have to possess a weapon to be safe you're in the wrong place. Very rarely do we go places unaware of the atmosphere or type of people who will be there. Being *"in the wrong places at the wrong time"* is not an excuse, because there's never *"a right time to be in the wrong place."* Trouble can break out anywhere at anytime, but the more information you know about the places you might find yourself, the better decisions you can make to avoid finding yourself in negative surroundings.

For example, I live in a neighborhood with three bodegas in a three-block radius. The bodega right across the street from my house is the one you can find people hanging out in front of at any given time of the day. The other two never have people hanging out in front of them, so to avoid having any potential negative confrontations with the people hanging in front of the closest bodega I go to one of the other two.

Things – The things you do to occupy your time is so very important. Idle time invites too much temptation to engage in negativity. People do all kinds of foolishness when bored or have nothing-constructive going on in their life. Find constructive things to occupy your time; school, work, a project, helping others, giving back to your community, involve yourself with a place of worship, workout, spend time with family or read a book are just a few things you can do can to keep yourself busy. When you are constantly busy you don't leave any room to indulge in unproductive, negative or destructive behaviors. When you have a plan and actively pursue your goals, there are countless things you can do to move you closer to them.

When you grow, you outgrow the old things that have been holding you back. You outgrow people, places, and things that were keeping you from being the best you can be and you outgrow the mindset that caused you to make poor choices.

Should people tell you they're wrongdoings when you come around?

_____

_____

_____

_____

Why will it be easy, hard or impossible to resist the temptation to go around the same "People, Places and Things" you did before going to prison?

_____

_____

_____

_____

Will it be easy, hard or impossible for you to find new "People, Places and Things" to surround yourself with after prison?

_____

_____

_____

_____

Name "People" you know you can't be around when you get out of prison.

✂ _____

✂ _____

✂ _____

✂ _____

✂ _____

✂ _____

Name "People" you know you can be around when you get out of prison.

✂ _____

✂ _____

✂ _____

✂ _____

✂ _____

✂ _____

List "Places" you know you can't go when you get out of prison.

✂ _____

✂ _____

✂ _____

✂ _____

✂ _____

✂ _____

List "Places" you know you can go when you get out of prison.

✂ _____

✂ _____

✂ _____

✂ _____

✂ _____

✂ _____

List "Things" you know you can't do when you get out of prison.

✂ _____

✂ _____

✂ _____

✂ _____

✂ _____

✂ _____

List "Things" you know you can do when you get out of prison.

✂ _____

✂ _____

✂ _____

✂ _____

✂ _____

✂ _____

Give an example of how people, places and things can jeopardize your freedom.

1. _____

_____

_____

2. _____

_____

_____

3. _____

_____

_____

Chapter afterthoughts

What did I get out of this chapter?

_____

_____

_____

_____

How can I apply this chapter to my life?

_____

_____

_____

What will I do differently now?

_____

_____

_____

What questions should have been asked in this chapter?

✂ _____

✂ _____

✂ _____

What can I add to this chapter to make it more powerful, engaging or helpful?

_____

_____

_____

_____

_____

Ballin' On A Budget

You absolutely have to include a budget plan in your new game plan. Budgeting money is something people have trouble with whether they've been incarcerated or not. As a street person, you never hear people talk about how to budget their money or how to live on a budget. Budgeting money is simply not a street concept. In the streets you make some money, you spend the money and then you're looking for or thinking up the next scheme to make more money. The money comes fast and it's gone even faster.

How does someone who has never lived on a budget learn how to budget his or her money now? Prison is teaching you how to budget your money whether you realize it or not. Most correctional facilities only allow inmates to spend a certain amount of money each month regardless of how much money is in their commissary account, so month-to-month inmates have to budget their money to make sure they have the things they need to survive. Sometimes people spend hours filling out a commissary slip figuring out how to get all the things needed using a small amount of money. It's in that weekly, bi-weekly, or monthly exercise you are learning how to budget your money.

When you get out, you're going to have to be budget conscious with your money. Before you went to prison you might have been the kind of individual who handled large sums of money so you never cared about a budget. Before, ten, twenty, and even fifty thousand dollars felt like a lot of money, when you get out having five hundred dollars in your hand gonna feel like a lot of money.

It's not how much money you make, its how much you save!

When you're released, any money you get has to go towards living expenses even when it means sacrificing things that are pleasurable to you. Food, rent, lights, gas, and carfare for work, hygiene items, and clothes become your main **priorities**. Your focus should be on the things you need vs. the things you want. Prison teaches you that as well. In prison you might want those brand new sneakers in commissary but those slightly used sneakers being sold in your housing unit will save you a nice chunk of change, so you make the sacrifice in order to buy your hygiene and food items.

More money more problems

The more your income increases the more the likely you will put less emphasis on sticking to your budget. This is where financial discipline will have to kick in. People often run into financial trouble because of their poor money management skills; not saving for a rainy day. Don't be that squirrel who played around all summer while all the other squirrels were looking for and stacking their acorns for the winter, because winter will come and you'll be one hungry squirrel, and we all know what hungry squirrels are capable of.

There are a few key reasons people fall short of their budgetary needs 1. Living above their means. 2. Depending on money they are supposed to get. 3. Poor money management skills.

Money management is much more then budgeting for your immediate needs upon release it's about creating a financial plan for your life. Unfortunately there's no financial retirement package when you retire from the streets. There's no **pension** plan, **401K** and for those who boast about never having worked a day in their life, there's no social security. Set a financial goal for yourself; where you want to be financially stable 5 to 10 years from now so you won't have to stress about how you're going to survive when you're a senior OG. Take the steps you need to take today that will get you where you want to be tomorrow.

Apply these budgetary approaches to your immediate release and long-term goals.
Monthly Income: $2,000.00

Expenses	Amount	Total
Home • Rent • Insurance	$600 $15	$615
Car • Insurance • Gas • Maintenance	$75 $80 $50	$205
Utilities • Electric bill • Water bill • Cell phone bill • Cable/internet	$30 $15 $45 $60	$150
Food • Groceries • Restaurants	$300 $50	$350
Personal • Clothes • Grooming • Medical	$60 $30 $50	$140
Other • Gifts • Entertainment	$50 $50	$100
	Total	$1,560

Income $2,000
- Expenses $1,560
           = $440 Unbudgeted income
           - $200 Flex money (10% of $2,000 monthly income)
           - $200 Savings (10% of $2,000 monthly income)
           = $40 **Surplus** to spend as you wish

Financial Literacy 101

Don't be that guy we see in most prison movies; the one who's handed $54.00 to start his life over with and a bus ticket home on the day of his release. You can begin to save for your future right now, doesn't matter you're in prison. At the end of my sentence I tried to calculate all the money I spent during my commissary and all I could think of was if I just saved half of the money I would be leaving prison with a nice little nest egg. In that sense I wasn't a very good steward of my finances during my incarceration.

I challenge you to save half the money you receive and/or make from your prison issued job starting now to begin building your prison release nest egg. Some prisons will help you setup a bank account. If you receive and/or make $100.00 a month spend $50.00 and save $50.00. If you do that each year of your sentence that will be $600.00 a year saved. You will appreciate this sacrifice when you walk out of prison with a nice piece of change to get your life started, trust me.

Establishing Credit

If you've never established credit or have messed up your credit I can't stress to you the importance of having good credit out here. Now jobs and almost all landlords run credit checks on people. Even some women might want to do a credit check on you. People use credit as a way to get a picture of the type of person you are. If you have poor credit, people will look at you as being irresponsible because you didn't keep your bills paid. And visa versa, good credit reflects positively on you and people see you can pay your bills on time.

Here are some simple steps you can take to get you on the road to establishing a credit history. Open a checking account with the first check you receive from your new job and deposit all your earnings for the next six weeks thereafter. Your bank will have a secured credit card plan you'll want to apply for after six weeks of depositing your earned income. A secured credit card only allows you to spend the amount on the card, but it's still accepted as a credit card everywhere you go. Put a minimum of 300 dollars on it. When you get the secured credit card, use it, but only pay a little over the minimum payment required each month to help establish your credit history. After making 4-6 payments on your secured credit card, apply for an instant credit card/account at any department store. You can walk right up to the cashier and fill out the application right there. After 8 months of using both your secured credit card and your store credit card, you can go to your bank and apply for a regular credit card.

Using these steps, you should be able to make a major credit purchase after 6-8 months. You can go to the bank and take out a small auto loan for the van you need to drive for a courier company. The thing about establishing credit is, YOU HAVE TO PAY YOUR BILLS ON TIME! You have to create a track record of being able to pay your bills. If you can do this after about 18 months your credit should be good enough for you to consider purchasing yourself a piece of property. There are so many programs out here that'll help put you in a house, condo or coop as long as your credit is good. Most of us never established credit so we're in a good position to create a strong credit score for ourselves.

From 1 – 10 what will go into your budget plan?

1. _____   6. _____

2. _____   7. _____

3. _____   8. _____

4. _____   9. _____

5. _____   10. _____

What are 3 consequences of not budgeting your money efficiently?

1. _____

2. _____

3. _____

How hard will it be for you to stick to your budget plan?

_____

_____

_____

Do criminals have budget plans? Yes ( ) No ( ) If not, why not?

_____

_____

There are two ways to meet your financial goals. One is to increase your income; the other is to decrease your expenses.

List ways you can increase your income ... legally.

✂ _____   ✂ _____

✂ _____   ✂ _____

✂ _____   ✂ _____

✂ _____   ✂ _____

What things you are willing to sacrifice to meet your budgetary needs?

✂ _____   ✂ _____

✂ _____   ✂ _____

✂ _____   ✂ _____

Why is important to have a great credit score?

_____

_____

_____

List ways you can damage your credit   **List ways you can fix your credit**

✂ _____   ✂ _____

✂ _____   ✂ _____

✂ _____   ✂ _____

List things you need credit to acquire or purchase?

✂ _____   ✂ _____

✂ _____   ✂ _____

✂ _____   ✂ _____

What is a credit report and what goes on it?

_____

_____

_____

What's the deference between a secured credit card and unsecured credit card?

_____

_____

_____

Chapter afterthoughts

What did I get out of this chapter?

_____

_____

_____

_____

How can I apply this chapter to my life?

_____

_____

_____

What will I do differently now?

_____

_____

_____

What questions should have been asked in this chapter?

✂ _____

✂ _____

✂ _____

What can I add to this chapter to make it more powerful, engaging or helpful?

_____

_____

_____

_____

_____

An Obligation to Change

One of the **obligations** each of you is faced with when you return to your community is making amends to the lives and communities you have helped destroy. A lot of us are the reason our neighborhoods are in the conditions they are in today. We were major contributors to the chaos, **mayhem,** and destruction **plaguing** our communities. When we were committing crime and living a lawless lifestyle, we never understood the impact and influence we had over the younger generation. We never stopped to think that a generation of young people would grow up, die and go to prison thinking that selling drugs, gangbanging, and being violent gave them self-worth.

It takes a village to raise a child.
-African Proverb
www.princesschrisy.com

Young people watched, imitated, and looked up to us as we came through wearing the expensive clothes, flashy jewelry, and driving the latest cars. They grew up **idolizing** the images of dope dealers, stickup men, and other criminal sorts, only to walk in the same street shoes as those they looked up to when they became young adults.

We are obligated to change so we can teach the younger generation the truth about the streets. Young people don't have a clue what's facing them when they choose this life. The saddest thing to see while incarcerated is a person young enough to be your son walking through the prison doors. We failed our youth in so many ways. We sold them the false illusions of street life and without our guidance, our sons and daughters are growing up with no direction.

Imagine the good you could do if you decide to influence young people positively. You could flip the script and teach youngsters the streets aren't cool, going to jail isn't cool, hustling isn't cool, and killing isn't cool. You can teach them beefs don't have to be dealt with violently. No matter how hard it might seem to reach the younger generation it's our obligation and duty to educate them, but the only way we can reach them is by being a living example of someone who made a positive change in life.

Because we contributed to the destruction of our communities, we should be the people who contribute to the building and uplifting of them now. As an act of redemption we have to start setting positive examples for our young people to follow. We have to start tearing down those false images of what cool and gangsta is, for starters. It's starts with each one of us, when each one of us starts taking responsibility to change our ways. It's time to go back to the time when we cared about our communities and the people in them. That place in time when you could go to your neighbor for a helping hand and everyone in the community looked out for one another.

Do you feel an obligation to change?

_____

_____

_____

Do you bare any responsibility for the destruction of your community?

_____

_____

_____

How can your change impact your community?

_____

_____

_____

What can you do to help others avoid the same mistakes you've made?

_____

_____

_____

What kind of changes would you like to be a part of in your community?

_____

_____

_____

How does glorifying prison/street life damage the community?

_____

_____

_____

What is something you can tell young people about prison to discourage them from going?

_____

_____

_____

What is something you can tell young people about the streets to discourage them from being in them?

_____

_____

_____

What is something you can tell young people about gangs to discourage them from joining?

_____

_____

_____

What is something you can tell young people about making poor choices to encourage them to make positive ones?

_____

_____

_____

Do you think people can redeem themselves?

_____

_____

_____

Name some people you don't want to wind up involved in the street?

_____   _____   _____

_____   _____   _____

Chapter afterthoughts

What did I get out of this chapter?

_____

_____

_____

_____

How can I apply this chapter to my life?

_____

_____

_____

What will I do differently now?

_____

_____

_____

What questions should have been asked in this chapter?

✂ _____

✂ _____

✂ _____

What can I add to this chapter to make it more powerful, engaging or helpful?

_____

_____

_____

_____

_____

Leaving A Legacy

Whether we work on leaving a **legacy** or not, every one of us is going to leave one. The only question is, what kind of legacy will it be? What mark will you leave on the world when your life on this earth is over? How will you be remembered? What will your tombstone read? What will you be remembered for? Ask yourself and be honest, *"if I died today what would my legacy be?"*

Would it be all-negative; jail, drugs, street schemes, mental incarceration? Would it be half negative and half positive? Would it be all positive? What will your legacy say about the way you treated people, family, friends, kids, **siblings**? Were you kind to your fellow man/woman? Consider these questions because you don't want to leave this life without leaving something that documents your time here.

Your legacy can be left in many ways. If you want to leave a legacy of excellence, strive to be your best every day, as you strive for **excellence** you will inspire excellence in others. If you want to leave a legacy of purpose make your life about something bigger than you, and if you want to leave a legacy of love live a life where your love is manifested in all the things you do.

We all die.

The goal isn't to live forever, the goal is to **create something that will.**

If your legacy would be very negative right now, it doesn't have to stay that way. You have the power to change the outcome of your legacy for the better. From this point forward live your life in a way that will leave a positive legacy for the ones who will remember you. Legacies are a **testament** to your life and a way to make some meaning of your existence. Each experience, challenge, trial, and tribulation adds to the content of your legacy. No one can create a legacy for you. Everyday you are alive offers you a new opportunity to work on your legacy.

A Financial Legacy – The things you have acquired throughout your life and have value to you are considered your estate. Your estate can consist of sentimental things like family **heirlooms** and other **mementos** and/or things that have monetary value like real-estate property, financial investments, savings, etc. You estate is what you leave your love ones when you pass away. Normally a person creates a will that explains how he or she wants their estate to be disposed of when he or she dies.

It's sad to say but most people who live and have lived the street life never leave a financial legacy. It's ironic that people spend most of their life trying to make a fast dollar, only to leave family and friends with the financial burden of their funeral when they pass because they did not even have a life insurance policy.

Have you ever thought about leaving a legacy? Why/why not?

_____

_____

_____

_____

Is leaving a legacy important to you? Why/why not?

_____

_____

_____

_____

Name 3 people who have left legacies and what were they?

1. _____

_____

2. _____

_____

3. _____

_____

How can your legacy impact/influence others?

_____

_____

_____

What would your legacy be right now today?

_____

_____

_____

What are 3 things you can do to ensure your legacy lives forever?

1. _____
   _____

2. _____
   _____

3. _____
   _____

How do you want people to remember you when you're gone?

_____

_____

_____

_____

Why can one wrong choice or bad decision ruin someone's legacy?

_____

_____

_____

_____

What are 3 things can you do to leave a financial legacy for your love ones?

1. _____
   _____

2. _____
   _____

3. _____
   _____

Chapter afterthoughts

What did I get out of this chapter?

_____

_____

_____

_____

How can I apply this chapter to my life?

_____

_____

_____

What will I do differently now?

_____

_____

_____

What questions should have been asked in this chapter?

✂ _____

✂ _____

✂ _____

What can I add to this chapter to make it more powerful, engaging or helpful?

_____

_____

_____

_____

_____

Time Management
(In Prison/On the Streets)

Time management means being accountable for your time, having something productive to show

for the minutes, hours, days, weeks, months, and years of your life. Every successful person knows time management is necessary even when it means cutting out activities in your life you enjoy to make time for the work needed to reach your goals.

Prison is probably one of the few times in your life, if at all; you are consciously reminded about time. Time becomes something that is constantly at the **forefront** of your mind. On the streets most of us lived outside the **constraints** of time, we came when we wanted, we left when we wanted and we did everything we wanted on our time. Time on the streets was measured in a series of events, not minutes, hours, or days. The few instances where the concept of time was real to us, was when we had a court date; you knew you had to be in that courtroom at 9:30am regardless what you were doing the night before. Another instance was right before, during, and as you made your escape from a crime scene, because you knew if you got caught you would be *facing time*. Most of us chose the street life because it gave us a sense of freedom to do what we wanted to do when we wanted to do it.

At the end of each day you should make an assessment of the day and ask yourself what did I do today, did I use the day productively? Did I spend time on the things that will move me closer to my goals? How much time did I waste today? How will I make better use of my time tomorrow? Your incarceration offers you a great opportunity to learn and **incorporate** time management into your new game plan.

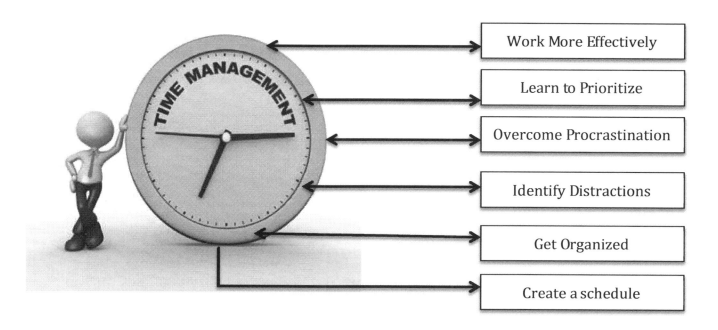

Time Management Budget Sheet

Total number of hours available each week   168

Minus hours in work each week   -_____

Minus hours of study time per week   -_____

Minus hours of sleep time/personal hygiene per week   -_____

Minus hours of committed time per week   -_____
(job, church, clubs, meetings)

Minus hours of meal time per week   -_____
(include coffee stops!)

Minus hours of exercise per week   -_____

Minus hours of family time per week

Minus hours of laundry, shopping, personal errands per week   -_____

Minus hours of television per week   -_____

Minus hours of Facebook, video games, etc.   -_____

Minus hours of other recreation per week (movies, parties, etc.)   -_____

Minus other (miscellaneous)   -_____

Final Balance (+ or -)   _____

     Incarceration is a **structured** environment, your movements are controlled in blocks of time and within those blocks of time, you have places to be or things you are required to be doing. If you're not where you're supposed to be, you can face disciplinary actions. Time management gives your life structure and having structure in your life is a good thing. It helps keep you mindful of your responsibilities and obligations. Without structure, we're wondering around not taking full advantage of our time. Having structure well help your goals be more attainable.

     Being late in prison doesn't have the same consequences as being late on the streets does. If you're late and miss the movement in prison you can get written up, you may lose your commissary privileges for a month or so, or you may lose your job. Being late on the streets can cost you, employment, a relationship, an opportunity, and more. On the streets lateness is a sign of being irresponsible. If you have to leave early to avoid being late, that's one less thing that can get in your way of success.

In prison all your time is accounted for, how could that same concept help you after prison?

_____

_____

_____

_____

People who are on time, make their appointments and manage how they spend your time, are normally....

✂ _____   ✂ _____

✂ _____   ✂ _____

✂ _____   ✂ _____

✂ _____   ✂ _____

✂ _____   ✂ _____

If you don't have enough time to do two things, how do you decide which one to do?

_____

_____

_____

What can lateness cost you and why?

_____

_____

_____

When traveling you should make allowances for what, to keep from being late?

_____

_____

_____

Why is time so valuable (even in prison)?

_____

_____

_____

List 5 things you can do to make better use of your time (in prison). Explain

1. _____

2. _____

3. _____

4. _____

5. _____

List 4 things you can do to make better use of your time (on the streets).

1. _____

2. _____

3. _____

4. _____

What are some ways that people waste time while in prison?

1. _____

2. _____

3. _____

Randy says, "It's not how much time you do; it's what you do with the time?" Is he right/wrong? Explain

_____

_____

_____

_____

Chapter afterthoughts

What did I get out of this chapter?

_____

_____

_____

_____

How can I apply this chapter to my life?

_____

_____

_____

_____

What will I do differently now?

_____

_____

_____

_____

What questions should have been asked in this chapter?

✂ _____

✂ _____

✂ _____

What can I add to this chapter to make it more powerful, engaging or helpful?

_____

_____

_____

_____

_____

Building a Support System

Even though we like to believe we can do everything on our own, we all need some form of help sometime from someone. If you have a strong support system in your corner upon your release it will help make your transition from prison a lot smoother than if you're going at it alone.

A support system is a group of people who are there to help you put the pieces of your life back together. Your support system is there to help prop you up until you're able to stand on your own feet. It's not suppose to take care of you forever. Each person in your support system can serve a useful purpose, from lending an ear to possibly lending you money for carfare, getting your necessary documents, etc.

Building a strong support system while in prison can be difficult but it is a very important piece of putting together your new game plan. You can start building your system by reaching out to your immediate family, closest friends, and then expand accordingly. Eventually you want to include people who share similar experiences as you so you have people in your support system who can relate to your challenges.

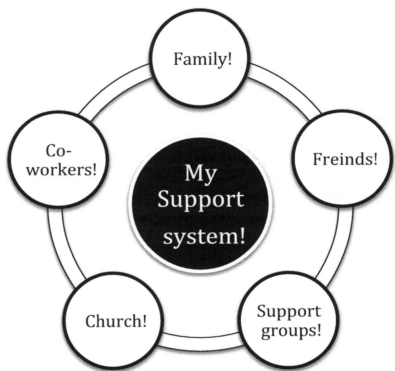

In the process of building your support system you may have to repair broken relationships with family and friends you burned bridges with prior to your incarceration. You have to be prepared for **initial** resistance to your efforts of reconciliation because you have lost people's trust. So the first order of business is trying to rebuild trust with the people you hurt. In order to have a strong support system, people have to be able to trust you. The only way you can get people to trust you again is by showing them you have changed.

You want positive people in your support system, people you can go to when you are feeling **overwhelmed** and **discouraged**. People who will talk you through a tough situation or guide you as you find your way after prison. People in your support system might be able to help you find a job, housing, or point you to resources that can help you with your immediate needs. What you don't want to do is become a burden on your support system, so remember they are there to help you not take care of you.

Why is it important to have a support system when you get released from prison?

_____

_____

_____

Who should be part of your support system?

_____

_____

_____

What kind of assistance can your support system give you?

_____

_____

_____

How can you lose the support of your support system?

_____

_____

_____

When should you go to your support system?

_____

_____

_____

How can you lose the support of your support system?

_____

_____

_____

List 5 people in your support system and what kind of support can they give you?

1. _____
2. _____
3. _____
4. _____
5. _____

What are 5 advantages of having a support system?

1. _____
2. _____
3. _____
4. _____
5. _____

What are 5 disadvantages of not having a support system?

1. _____
2. _____
3. _____
4. _____
5. _____

Can a person go through life without needing someone at some point? Explain

_____

_____

_____

_____

Chapter afterthoughts

What did I get out of this chapter?

_____

_____

_____

_____

How can I apply this chapter to my life?

_____

_____

_____

What will I do differently now?

_____

_____

_____

What questions should have been asked in this chapter?

✂ _____

✂ _____

✂ _____

What can I add to this chapter to make it more powerful, engaging or helpful?

_____

_____

_____

_____

Incarcerated On Paper

Incarcerated on paper means being on parole, probation, or some sort of court ordered supervision (usually following your incarceration). In order to avoid running **afoul** of your supervision conditions it's best to know exactly what is expected of you as soon as you meet with your parole officer. Keep in mind you're still incarcerated you're just not surrounded by barbwire and fences, so follow all your conditions to the letter.

There's nothing wrong with trying to establish a good relationship with your parole or probation officer. It's counter productive to see your P.O as the enemy when his/her job is too make sure you meet your supervision conditions. Most people tend to blame their P.O for violating their parole, instead of looking at the reasons they gave the P.O. to violate them in the first place. In some cases you might run into a P.O. who seems extremely hard on his/her clients and looks for any little thing to send them back to prison on a violation. So understanding that, it is your job to make sure you don't give your P.O. a reason to violate you.

If you need to travel, you ask for permission. You need to move, you notify your P.O. you moved. You have programs to report to, report. You have to get a job, provide the P.O. with a paper trail of your job searches. You have a curfew, meet your curfew.

If you're having a problem or a **foreseeable** problem with a spouse, girlfriend/boyfriend, baby momma or baby father talk to your P.O. about it in advance, don't wait until a situation **escalates** and explodes and then try to explain your side of the story, it may be too late then. Get out in front of all potential negative situations that can jeopardize your freedom, first red flag or warning sign you get.

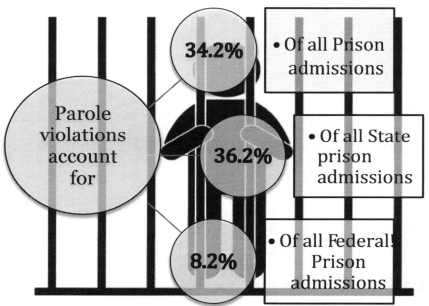

Parole violations account for

34.2% • Of all Prison admissions

36.2% • Of all State prison admissions

8.2% • Of all Federal Prison admissions

Like it or not, your P.O. holds the keys to your freedom in his/her hands. You can establish a good relationship with your P.O. by sharing and following through with your plans.

If you follow the conditions that have been set for you, then you leave no reasons for violation. Show your P.O. you're serious about building a positive life for yourself and 9 times out of 10 he/she will support you. In that one remaining case, it's still up to you to follow through with your plans and don't give your P.O. a reason to violate you. P.O's love clients who don't give them any headaches, it makes their job easier. If you become a headache for your P.O. eventually he/she will find a way and a reason to shut you down, and you know what that means.

What are a few things you can do to successfully complete your parole?

✂ _____

✂ _____

✂ _____

What parole conditions do you find unreasonable?

✂ _____   ✂ _____

✂ _____   ✂ _____

✂ _____   ✂ _____

List reasons a "technical violation" (non arrested) can send you back to prison.

✂ _____   ✂ _____

✂ _____   ✂ _____

✂ _____   ✂ _____

What is the advantage of having a positive relationship with your P.O.?

_____

_____

_____

What will you do if you get a parole officer who seems hard on you?

_____

_____

_____

How can you build a good relationship with your parole officer?

_____

_____

_____

Chapter afterthoughts

What did I get out of this chapter?

_____

_____

_____

_____

How can I apply this chapter to my life?

_____

_____

_____

What will I do differently now?

_____

_____

_____

What questions should have been asked in this chapter?

✂ _____

✂ _____

✂ _____

What can I add to this chapter to make it more powerful, engaging or helpful?

_____

_____

_____

_____

_____

_____

Creating A New Game Plan

As you create a new game plan for your life, your game plan has to be **flexible** because there are times you'll have to adjust and re-adjust in accordance to daily events. Your game plan is your roadmap to success; it lays out what the plan is and how you plan to make it a reality. It's a written document that puts into words what you want out of life and defines your **objectives**.

The first step to creating your new game plan is considering what you want to achieve. Setting short-term, long-term and lifetime goals gives you the overall perspective that shapes all other **aspects** of your decision-making. The next step is assembling the resources necessary to achieve your plan and the last step is the **implementation** of your game plan.

A great way to create your new game is to put together a vision board. A vision board is a collage of images, pictures, and affirmations of your dreams, goals, and things that make you happy. Creating a vision board can be a useful tool to help you conceptualize your goals and can serve as a source of motivation as you work towards achieving your dreams.

Before starting your vision board, spend time thinking about what your goals are, what kind of life you want to live and what's most important to you. You can create as many vision boards as you want, each with a different theme.

Vision boards are physical boards made out of poster-board, corkboard, or any material that can be hung on or propped against a wall that will allow you to view the vision board regularly and reflect upon it daily. Because there's a restriction on hanging things (like a vision board) on walls in prison you will have to improvise when creating your *vision board*.

Vision board, prison style — Purchase a photo album from the commissary and use the pages in your photo album to create your vision book. Collect inspirational images and inspiring quotes for your vision book, be creative with your arrangement. Your vision book will serve as a private source of inspiration so pull it out and look at it every day. Your vision book can keep you focused and motivated.

Use your vision book to visualize the process of achieving success, not just the result. A lot of people get caught up fantasizing about the end results and not the work needed to get the end results. Your vision book should be a blueprint with minute details of everything you need and need to do to be successful, not a vision book that mainly focuses on celebrating your success. A vision is when you actually visual everything it will take to make the vision a reality.

Vision Book themes —

- Healthy Relationships
- Career/Job
- Entrepreneurial
- Positive Living

Creating a new game plan will help me...

_____

_____

_____

_____

Things I am Great at Doing
Ex. Getting things done, showing up on time, paying attention to details

✂ _____   ✂ _____

✂ _____   ✂ _____

✂ _____   ✂ _____

My Skills and Talents
Ex. Fixing cars, gardening, cooking, drawing, writing

✂ _____   ✂ _____

✂ _____   ✂ _____

✂ _____   ✂ _____

Skills I need to develop
Ex. Take class on plumbing, learn how to fix computers, get CDL license

✂ _____   ✂ _____

✂ _____   ✂ _____

✂ _____   ✂ _____

Things I need to do or learn that will strengthen my future
Ex. How to use Standard English in my writing. How to type. Use the computer.

✂ _____   ✂ _____

✂ _____   ✂ _____

✂ _____   ✂ _____

3 Things I must do on the outside
Ex. Contact publishers, get CDL license, enroll in college

1. _____

2. _____

3. _____

Why is it so important to get your state ID card immediately?

_____

_____

_____

How/where do you get the following documents/services where you?

Birth certificate _____

Social Security Card _____

State Identification _____

Driver's License _____

Food Stamps _____

Public Assistance _____

Health Care _____

What are some of the things I need to implement my new game plan?
Ex: Support, Resources, Finances, Patience etc.

✂ _____   ✂ _____

✂ _____   ✂ _____

✂ _____   ✂ _____

What are the consequences of not staying focused on my plan?

_____

_____

Chapter afterthoughts

What did I get out of this chapter?

_____

_____

_____

_____

How can I apply this chapter to my life?

_____

_____

_____

What will I do differently now?

_____

_____

_____

What questions should have been asked in this chapter?

✂ _____

✂ _____

✂ _____

What can I add to this chapter to make it more powerful, engaging or helpful?

_____

_____

_____

_____

_____

The First 72

The first 72 hours of release are critical to your success. If you can check some of these "things to do" off your list before your release that's great, if not, creating a checklist still gives you the advantage of upon your release.

Contact my immediate family
Mother/Father/Children/Wife

_____

_____

Report to the Parole/Probations Office
(Usually want do this in first 24 hours)

_____

_____

Get State Identification, Birth Certificate,
Social Security Card

_____

_____

Apply for Social Services; Food Stamps,
Cash Assistance, Medicaid Assistance, Etc.

_____

_____

Contact local Prison Reentry Programs

_____

_____

Visit library for your computer needs
and reentry resource information

_____

_____

Now I have all my documents I can start looking for employment, my next move is....

- Visit local library – Get Library card to access computers. Ask about resources for formerly incarcerated people.
- Create an email account Create a resume. Google resumes and you create a resume in minutes online
- Visit www.craigslist.org for day labor jobs and other opportunities
- Do online job search, fill out job applications online

Notes to myself

_____

_____

_____

_____

_____

My 30 Day Plan

CAREER
What do I want to achieve? _____

Steps I'm taking to achieve this goal

    1. _____

    2. _____

    3. _____

FINANCIAL
What do I want to achieve? _____

Steps I'm taking to achieve this goal.

    1. _____

    2. _____

    3. _____

PERSONAL
What do I want to achieve? _____

Steps I'm taking to achieve this goal.

    1. _____

    2. _____

    3. _____

FAMILY
What do I want to achieve? _____

Steps I'm taking to achieve this goal

    1. _____

    2. _____

    3. _____

    4. _____

HEALTH

What do I want to achieve? _____

Steps I'm taking to achieve this goal.

    1. _____

    2. _____

    3. _____

RELATIONALSHIP

What do I want to achieve? _____

Steps I'm taking to achieve this goal.

    1. _____

    2. _____

    3. _____

Miscellaneous

What do I want to achieve? _____

Steps I'm taking to achieve this goal.

    1. _____

    2. _____

    3. _____

Notes to myself

_____

_____

_____

_____

_____

_____

_____

My 6 Months Plan

CAREER
What do I want to achieve? _____

Steps I'm taking to achieve this goal

    1. _____

    2. _____

    3. _____

FINANCIAL
What do I want to achieve? _____

Steps I'm taking to achieve this goal.

    1. _____

    2. _____

    3. _____

PERSONAL
What do I want to achieve? _____

Steps I'm taking to achieve this goal.

    1. _____

    2. _____

    3. _____

FAMILY
What do I want to achieve? _____

Steps I'm taking to achieve this goal

    1. _____

    2. _____

    3. _____

    4. _____

HEALTH

What do I want to achieve? _____

Steps I'm taking to achieve this goal.

    1. _____

    2. _____

    3. _____

RELATIONALSHIP

What do I want to achieve? _____

Steps I'm taking to achieve this goal.

    1. _____

    2. _____

    3. _____

Miscellaneous

What do I want to achieve? _____

Steps I'm taking to achieve this goal.

    1. _____

    2. _____

    3. _____

Notes to myself

_____

_____

_____

_____

_____

_____

My 1 Year Plan

CAREER
What do I want to achieve? _____

Steps I'm taking to achieve this goal

1. _____

2. _____

3. _____

FINANCIAL
What do I want to achieve? _____

Steps I'm taking to achieve this goal.

1. _____

2. _____

3. _____

PERSONAL
What do I want to achieve? _____

Steps I'm taking to achieve this goal.

1. _____

2. _____

3. _____

FAMILY
What do I want to achieve? _____

Steps I'm taking to achieve this goal

1. _____

2. _____

3. _____

4. _____

HEALTH
What do I want to achieve? _____

Steps I'm taking to achieve this goal.

    1. _____

    2. _____

    3. _____

RELATIONALSHIP
What do I want to achieve? _____

Steps I'm taking to achieve this goal.

    1. _____

    2. _____

    3. _____

Miscellaneous
What do I want to achieve? _____

Steps I'm taking to achieve this goal.

    1. _____

    2. _____

    3. _____

Notes to myself

_____

_____

_____

_____

_____

_____

My 3 Year Plan

CAREER
What do I want to achieve? _____

Steps I'm taking to achieve this goal

    1. _____

    2. _____

    3. _____

FINANCIAL
What do I want to achieve? _____

Steps I'm taking to achieve this goal.

    1. _____

    2. _____

    3. _____

PERSONAL
What do I want to achieve? _____

Steps I'm taking to achieve this goal.

    1. _____

    2. _____

    3. _____

FAMILY
What do I want to achieve? _____

Steps I'm taking to achieve this goal

    1. _____

    2. _____

    3. _____

    4. _____

HEALTH
What do I want to achieve? _____

Steps I'm taking to achieve this goal.

     1. _____

     2. _____

     3. _____

RELATIONALSHIP
What do I want to achieve? _____

Steps I'm taking to achieve this goal.

     1. _____

     2. _____

     3. _____

Miscellaneous
What do I want to achieve? _____

Steps I'm taking to achieve this goal.

     1. _____

     2. _____

     3. _____

Notes to myself

_____

_____

_____

_____

_____

_____

My 5 Year Plan

CAREER
What do I want to achieve? _____

Steps I'm taking to achieve this goal

    4. _____

    5. _____

    6. _____

FINANCIAL
What do I want to achieve? _____

Steps I'm taking to achieve this goal.

    4. _____

    5. _____

    6. _____

PERSONAL
What do I want to achieve? _____

Steps I'm taking to achieve this goal.

    4. _____

    5. _____

    6. _____

FAMILY
What do I want to achieve? _____

Steps I'm taking to achieve this goal

    5. _____

    6. _____

    7. _____

    8. _____

HEALTH
What do I want to achieve? _____

Steps I'm taking to achieve this goal.

4. _____

5. _____

6. _____

RELATIONALSHIP
What do I want to achieve? _____

Steps I'm taking to achieve this goal.

4. _____

5. _____

6. _____

Miscellaneous
What do I want to achieve? _____

Steps I'm taking to achieve this goal.

4. _____

5. _____

6. _____

Notes to myself

_____

_____

_____

_____

_____

_____

My Lifetime Plan

CAREER
What do I want to achieve? _____

Steps I'm taking to achieve this goal

    7. _____

    8. _____

    9. _____

FINANCIAL
What do I want to achieve? _____

Steps I'm taking to achieve this goal.

    7. _____

    8. _____

    9. _____

PERSONAL
What do I want to achieve? _____

Steps I'm taking to achieve this goal.

    7. _____

    8. _____

    9. _____

FAMILY
What do I want to achieve? _____

Steps I'm taking to achieve this goal

    9. _____

    10. _____

    11. _____

    12. _____

HEALTH
What do I want to achieve? _____

Steps I'm taking to achieve this goal.

7. _____

8. _____

9. _____

RELATIONALSHIP
What do I want to achieve? _____

Steps I'm taking to achieve this goal.

7. _____

8. _____

9. _____

Miscellaneous
What do I want to achieve? _____

Steps I'm taking to achieve this goal.

7. _____

8. _____

9. _____

Notes to myself

_____

_____

_____

_____

_____

_____

Stages of Learning a New Word

4 Can USE IT in Speaking and Writing

3 General association or recognizes in context

2 Heard it, but don't know what it means

1 Never heard it or saw it before

Introduction

Consequence *noun*
- The effect, result, or outcome of something occurring earlier.
- An act or instance of following something as an effect, result, or outcome.

Practical *adj.*
- Of, relating to, or concerned with ordinary activities, business, or work.
- Adapted or designed for actual use.

Transitioning *noun*
- Movement, passage, or change from onep osition,state, stage, subject, concept,etc., to another; change.

Complex *adj.*
- Composed of many interconnected parts; compound; composite.
- Characterized by a very complicated or in volved arrangement of parts, units, etc.
- So complicated or intricate as to be hard to understand or deal with.

Author's Biography

Entrenched –!*adj.*
- (Of an attitude, habit, or belief) firmly established and difficult or unlikely to change; ingrained.

Scraggly – *adj,*
- Growing in a way that is not neat and even, having a ragged appearance.

Vile – *adj.*
- Evil or immoral: Very bad or unpleasant.

Forged – *noun*
- To form or bring into being especially by an expenditure of effort

Slew - *noun*
- A large amount or number.

Dysfunctional – *noun*
- The condition of having poor and unhealthy behaviors and attitudes within a group of people.

Redemption – *noun*
- The act of saving people from sin and evil: the fact of being saved from sin or evil.

Adversity – *noun*
- A difficult situation or condition,
- Misfortune or tragedy.

Preparing for Success

Staggering – *adjective*
- Very large, shocking, or surprising.

Degradation – *noun*
- The act of treating someone or something poorly and without respect.

Investment *noun*
- A devoting, using, or giving of time, talent or emotional energy, etc., as for a purpose or to achieve something.

Components - *noun*
- One of the parts of something (such as a system or mixture): an important piece of something.

Equation - *noun*
- A complex of variable factors.

Frivolous - *adj.*
- Not serious in content or attitude or behavior.

Hypothetical - *adj.*
- Based primarily on surmise rather than adequate evidence; *noun* a hypothetical possibility, circumstance, statement, proposal, situation, etc.

What is Change?

Striving - *intransitive verb*
- To try very hard to do or achieve something.

Circumstances – *noun*
- An event or situation that you cannot control, the way something happens, the specific details of an event.

Resistant – *adj.*
- Opposed to something: wanting to prevent something from happening.

Acknowledge – *verb*
- To say that you accept or do not deny the truth or existence of (something).

Triggers - *noun*
- Something that causes something else to happen.

Gap – *noun*
- A space between two people or things.

The Journey to Self-Discovery

Consciously – *adverb*
- Done or acting with critical awareness.

Empowering – *verb*
- To promote the self-actualization or influence of.

Awakening – *verb,*
- To stop sleeping, to wake up.

Constructive – *adj.*
- Helping to develop or improve something.

Passion – *noun*
- A strong feeling of enthusiasm or excitement for something or about doing something

Passionate – *adj.*
- Having, showing, or expressing strong emotions or beliefs.

Dignity *noun*
- Bearing, conduct, or speech indicative of self-respect or appreciation of the formality or gravity of an occasion or situation.

Insurmountable – *adj.*
- Of a problem, difficulty, etc.: impossible to solve or get control of: impossible to overcome.

Self-Improvement

Chaos – *noun*
- Complete confusion and disorder: a state in which behavior and events are not controlled by anything.

Unresolved – *adjective*
- Of a problem, question, or dispute not resolved.

Evaluate *verb*
- To judge the value or condition of (someone or something) in a careful and thoughtful way.

Critical – *adj.*
- Using or involving careful judgment about the good and bad parts of something

Discipline – *noun*
- A way of behaving that shows a willingness to obey rules or orders.

Potential – *adj.*
- Existing in possibility, capable of development into actuality.

Outweighs – *verb*
- To be greater than (someone or something) in weight, value, or importance.

Cultivate – *verb*
- Grow or nurture (something) under conditions that you can control.

Superficial – *adj.*
- Concerned only with what is obvious or apparent, not thorough or complete.

Facades – *noun*
- A way of behaving or appearing that gives other people a false idea of your true feelings or situation.

Analyze – *verb*
- To study (something) closely and carefully: to learn the nature and relationship of the parts of (something) by a close and careful examination.

Playing The (so-called) Game

Flipside – noun
- The bad or unpleasant part or result of something.

Fictitious – *adj.*
- Of relating to, or characteristic of <u>fiction</u>, imaginary.

Illusion – *noun*
- Something that looks or seems different from what it is, something that is false or not real but that seems to be true or real.

Gravitates – *verb*
- To move or tend to move to or toward someone or something.

Diminishes – *verb*
- To become or to cause (something) to become less in size, importance, etc.

Brainwash – *noun*
- A forcible indoctrination to induce someone to give up basic political, social, or religious beliefs and attitudes and to accept contrasting regimented ideas.

Romanticized – *verb*
- To think about or describe something as being better or more attractive or interesting than it really is: to show, describe, or think about something in a romantic way.

Reminiscing - *verb*
- To talk, think, or write about things that happened in the past.

Mentally Incarcerated

Obstacle — *noun*
- Something that makes it difficult to do something.

Exacerbates *verb*
- To increase the severity, bitterness, or violence of(disease, ill feeling, etc.); aggravate.

Indoctrinated *verb*
- To instruct in a doctrine, principle, ideology, etc.,especially to imbue with a specific partisan or biased belief or point of view.

Psyche - *noun*
- The soul, mind, or personality of a person or group.

Warped — *noun*
- A twist or curve in something that is usually flat or straight.

Rationales - *noun*
- The reason or explanation for something

Exhilarating - *adj.*
- Making lively and cheerful; making lively and joyful.

Pilgrimages - *noun*
- A journey to a sacred place.

Institutionalized

Isolated - *adj.*
- Cut off or left behind; remote and separate physically or socially; being or feeling set or kept apart from others.

Devoid - *adj.*
- Completely lacking; completely wanting or lacking.

Process - *noun*
- A continuous action, operation, or or series of changes taking place in a definite manner.

Exhibit - *verb*
- Show an attribute, property, knowledge, or skill; to show, make visible or apparent; show or demonstrate something to an interested audience.
-

Dependency - *noun*
- Lack of independence or self-sufficiency; being abnormally tolerant to and dependent on something that is psychologically or physically habit-forming (especially alcohol or narcotic drugs).

Spontaneity - *noun*
- The quality of being spontaneous and coming from natural feelings without constraint.

Monotony - *noun*
- The quality of wearisome constancy, routine, and lack of variety.

Mechanisms — *noun*
- The agency or means by which an effect is produced or a purpose is accomplished.

Getting Your Mind right

Scenarios - *noun*
- A postulated sequence of possible events.

Impulse - *noun*
- A sudden desire; an instinctive motive.

Overwhelmed - *verb*
- Charge someone with too many tasks; overcome, as with emotions or perceptual stimuli.

Swayed - *noun*
- Controlling influence; pitching dangerously to one side; *verb* move back and forth or sideways; win approval or support for.

Sabotage - *noun*
- A deliberate act of destruction or disruption in which equipment is damaged; *verb* destroy property or hinder normal operations.

Detoxify *verb*
- To rid of poison or the effect of poison.
- To treat (a person addicted to alcohol or d rugs) under a program of <u>detoxification</u>.
-

Interpret *verb*
- To give or provide the meaning of.
- Explain; explicate; elucidate.
- To construe or understand in a particular way.

Playing Catch Up

Stagnate - *verb*
- Cease to flow; stand without moving; cause to stagnate; stand still; be idle; exist in a changeless situation.

Concept - *noun*
- An abstract or general idea inferred or derived from specific instances.

Immensely - *adv.*
- To an exceedingly great extent or degree.

Grievance - *noun*
- A complaint about a (real or imaginary) wrong that causes resentment and is grounds for action.

Attitude Adjustment

Vain - *adj.*
- Unproductive of success; characteristic of false pride; having an exaggerated sense of self-importance.

Passport - *noun*
- A document issued by a country to a citizen allowing that person to travel abroad and re-enter the home country.

Hinge - *noun*
- A circumstance upon which subsequent events depend.

Embark - *verb*
- Set out on (an enterprise or subject of study); go on board; proceed somewhere despite the risk of possible dangers.

Optimistic - *adj.*
- Expecting the best in this best of all possible worlds; expecting the best.

Pessimistic - *adj.*
- Expecting the worst in this worst of all possible worlds.

Overcoming Bitterness

Bitter - *adj.*
- Proceeding from or exhibiting great hostility or animosity; expressive of severe grief or regret; marked by strong resentment or cynicism; harsh or corrosive in tone.

Fester (ed) - *noun*
- A sore that has become inflamed and formed pus; *verb,* ripen and generate pus.

Ferment (ed) - *noun*
- A state of agitation or turbulent change or development; *verb* cause to undergo fermentation; work up into agitation or excitement; be in an agitated or excited state; go sour or spoil.

Spiral - *verb*
- Flying downward in a helical path with a large radius; form a spiral; to wind or move in a spiral course; move in a spiral or zigzag course.

Abandonment - *noun*
- The act of giving something up; withdrawing support or help despite allegiance or responsibility.

Dwell - *verb*
- Think moodily or anxiously about something; come back to.

Facilitate - *verb*
- Make easier; increase the likelihood of (a response); be of use.

Reconciliation - *noun*
- Getting two things to correspond; the reestablishing of cordial relations.

Anger Management

Fleeting - *adj.*
- Lasting for a markedly brief time.

Minefield - *noun*
- A region in which explosives mines have been placed.

Brisk - *adj.*
- Very active; quick and energetic; imparting vitality and energy; *verb* become brisk.

Confrontational - *adj.*
- Of or relating to confrontation.

Stress Management

Synonymous - *adj.*
- (Of words) meaning the same or nearly the same.

Rigor - *noun*
- Excessive sternness; something hard to endure; the quality of being logically valid.

Indulge - *verb*
- Enjoy to excess; give free rein to; yield (to); give satisfaction to; treat with excessive indulgence.

Diversions - *noun*
- A turning aside (of your course or attention or concern); an activity that diverts or amuses or stimulates; an attack calculated to draw enemy defense away from the point of the principal attack.

Alleviate - *verb*
- Provide physical relief, as from pain; make easier.

Changing Your Perspective

Perspective - *noun*
- A way of regarding situations or topics etc.

Values - *noun*
- Beliefs of a person or social group in which they have an emotional investment (either for or against something).

Principle - *noun*
- A basic truth or law or assumption; a rule or law concerning a natural phenomenon or the function of a complex system; a basic generalization that is accepted as true and that can be used as a basis for reasoning or conduct.
- A rule or standard especially of good behavior; rule of personal conduct.

Interpretation - *noun*
- An explanation of something that is not immediately obvious; an explanation that results from interpreting something.

Analogy - *noun*
- Drawing a comparison in order to show a similarity in some respect.

Motivation 101

Motivation - *noun*
- The reason for the action; that which gives purpose and direction to behavior; the act of motivating; providing incentive; the condition of being motivated

Self-esteem - *noun*
- A feeling of pride in yourself; the quality of being worthy of esteem or respect

Correlation - *noun*
- A reciprocal relation between two or more things; a statistic representing how closely two variables co-vary

Inevitable - *adj.*
- Incapable of being avoided or prevented; invariably occurring or appearing; *noun* an unavoidable event.
-

Commitment - *noun*
- The act of committing.
- The state of being committed.
- The act of committing, pledging or engaging oneself.
- A pledge or promise; obligation.

Discipline - *noun*
- Training to act in accordance with rules; drill.
- Activity, exercise, or a regimen that develops or improves a skill; training.
- Behavior in accord with rules of conduct.

Perseverance - *noun*
- Steady persistence in a course of action, a purpose, a state, etc., especially in spite of difficulties, obstacles, or discouragement

Sacrifice 101

Sacrifice - *noun*
- Surrendered or lost in order to gain an objective; a loss entailed by giving up or selling something at less than its value; the act of losing or surrendering something as a penalty for a mistake or fault or failure to perform.

Obligated - *adj.*
- Caused by law or conscience to follow a certain course.

Appreciate - *verb*
- Recognize with gratitude; be grateful for; hold dear.

Monetarily adj.
- Of or relating to money or currency.

Unwavering - *adj.*
- Marked by firm determination or resolution; not shakable; not showing abrupt variations.

Focus 101

Mode - *noun*
- A manner of acting or doing; method.
- A particular type or form of something.

Euphoria - *noun*
- a state of intense happiness and self-confidence
- *Psychology* a feeling of happiness, confidence, or well-being sometimes exaggerated in pathological states.

Contribute - *verb*
- Contribute to some cause; be conducive to; provide; bestow a quality on.

Squandered - *adj.*
- Not used to good advantage; wasted.

A Mother's Pain

Comprehend - *verb*
- To understand the nature or meaning of; grasp with the mind; perceive.

Depth - *noun*
- Degree of psychological or intellectual profundity; the intellectual ability to penetrate deeply into ideas.

Dread(ed) verb
- To fear greatly; be in extreme apprehension.
- To be reluctant to do, meet, or experience

40 Years old (running out of time)

- **Imperative** - *adj.* requiring attention or action; relating to verbs in the imperative mood;
- *noun* some duty that is essential and urgent; a mood that expresses an intention to influence the listener's behavior.

Overcoming Hopelessnes

Hopelessness - *noun*
- The despair you feel when you have abandoned hope of comfort or success.

Dreariness - *noun*
- Extreme dullness; lacking spirit or interest.

Alienated - *adj.*
- Caused to be unloved; socially disoriented.

Forsake - *verb*
- Leave someone who needs or counts on you; leave in the lurch.

Uninspired - *adj.*
- Having no intellectual or emotional or spiritual excitement; deficient in originality or creativity; lacking powers of invention.

Fixate - *verb*
- Become fixed (on); make fixed, stable or stationary; pay attention to exclusively and obsessively; attach (oneself) to a person or thing in a neurotic way.

Staying Sucker Free

Ecstatic - *adj.*
- Feeling great rapture or delight

Instigate - *verb*
- Serve as the inciting cause of; provoke or stir up

Masquerading - *noun*
- False outward show; façade; pretense:
- Activity, existence, etc., under false pretenses.

Significant other *noun*
- A person with whom someone has an established romantic or sexual relationship.

Playing the Blame Game

Resolve - *noun*
- The trait of being resolute; bring to an end; settle conclusively.
-

Responsibility - *noun*
- A form of trustworthiness; the trait of being answerable to someone for something or being responsible for one's conduct.

Deflect - *verb*
- Turn aside and away from an initial or intended course; draw someone's attention away from something; prevent the occurrence of.

Demise - *noun*
- The time when something ends.

External - *adj.*
- Happening or arising or located outside or beyond some limits or especially surface; purely outward or superficial.

Onward - *adj.*
- Moving toward a position ahead; *adv.* in a forward direction; forward in time or order or degree

Prison: The Life Saving Factor

Eventuality - *noun*
- A contingent event; a possible occurrence or circumstance.

Fate - *noun*
- An event (or a course of events) that will inevitably happen in the future.
- Your overall circumstances or condition in life (including everything that happens to you).
- *verb* decree or designate beforehand

Escalate - *verb*
- Increase in extent or intensity

Perceived - *adj.*
- Detected by means of the senses; detected by instinct or inference rather than by recognized perceptual cues.

Infinite - *adj.*
- Having no limits or boundaries in time or space or extent or magnitude; too numerous to be counted; *noun* the unlimited expanse in which everything is located.

Despised - *adj.*
- Treated with contempt.

Manipulator - *noun*
- Control (others or oneself) or influence skillfully, influence or control shrewdly or deviously.

Relationships 101

Core - *noun*
- The choicest or most essential or most vital part of some idea or experience; the central meaning or theme of a speech or literary work.

Integrity - *noun*
- Moral soundness; an undivided or unbroken completeness or totality with nothing wanting.

Reconcile - *verb*
- Come to terms; bring into consonance or accord; make compatible with; accept as inevitable.

Remorse - *noun*
- A feeling of deep regret (usually for some misdeed).

Consistency - *noun*
- A harmonious uniformity or agreement among things or parts; (logic) an attribute of a logical system that is so constituted that none of the propositions deducible from the axioms contradict one another.

Gauge - *noun*
- Measure precisely and against a standard; determine the capacity, volume, or contents of by measurement and calculation; judge tentatively or form an estimate of (quantities or time).

Healthy Romantic Relationship

Beneficial - *adj.*
- Promoting or enhancing well-being; tending to promote physical well-being; beneficial to health.

Potentially - *adv.*
- With a possibility of becoming actual.

Considerate - *adj.*
- Showing concern for the rights and feelings of others.

Compatibility - *noun*
- Capability of existing or performing in harmonious or congenial combination; a feeling of sympathetic understanding.

Intimacy - *noun*
- Close or warm friendship; a feeling of being intimate and belonging together; a usually secretive or illicit sexual relationship.

Jaded - *adj.*
- Dulled by surfeit; exhausted.

Nurture - *noun* (nurturing)
- Helping someone grow up to be an accepted member of the community;
- *verb* help develop, help grow; provide with nourishment; bring up.

Endeavor - *noun*
- Earnest and conscientious activity intended to do or accomplish something; a purposeful or industrious undertaking (especially one that requires effort or boldness); *verb* attempt by employing effort

Strife - *noun*
- Bitter conflict heated often violent dissension; lack of agreement or harmony.

Prison Parenting

Parental - *adj.*
- Relating to or characteristic of or befitting a parent.

Exert - *verb*
- Make a great effort at a mental or physical task; have and exercise.

Authoritarian - *adj.*
- Characteristic of an absolute ruler or absolute rule; having absolute sovereignty; expecting unquestioning obedience; likened to a dictator in severity.
- *noun* a person who behaves in an tyrannical manner.

Resentment - *noun*
- A feeling of deep and bitter anger and ill-will.

Manifest - *adj.*
- Clearly revealed to the mind or the senses or judgment; *verb* stand as proof of; show by one's behavior, attitude, or external attributes.

Deterrent - *adj.*
- Tending to deter; *noun* something immaterial that interferes with or delays action or progress.

Milestone - *noun*
- A significant event in your life (or in a project).

Transparent - *adj.*
- Easily understood or seen through (because of a lack of subtlety); transmitting light; free of deceit.

Mandated - *noun*
- An authoritative order or command

Overcoming Addiction

Compulsive - *adj.*
- Caused by or suggestive of psychological compulsion; *noun* a person with a compulsive disposition; someone who feels compelled to do certain things.

Interferes - *verb*
- Come between so as to be hindrance or obstacle; get involved, so as to alter or hinder an action, or through force or threat of force.

Inability - *noun*
- Lacking the power to perform; lack of ability (especially mental ability) to do something.

Irrational - *adj.*
- Not consistent with or using reason.

Trapping - *noun*
- Outward decoration or dress; ornamental equipment.

Steadily - *adv.*
- At a steady rate or pace; in a steady manner.

Vow (ing) - *noun*
- A solemn pledge (to oneself or to another or to a deity)
- *verb* make a vow; promise

A Traumatized Life

Traumatic
- Of, relating to, or produced by a trauma or wound.
- Psychologically painful.

Withdrawn - *verb*
- past participle of withdraw.
- Removed from circulation, contact, competition, etc.
- Shy; retiring; reticent.

Nothin' Sweet 'Bout Prison

Create Comforts – *adj.*
- Luxuries; amenities.

Lull - *noun*
- A pause during which things are calm or activities are diminished; *verb* become quiet or less intensive; calm by deception; make calm or still

Subconsciously - *adv.*
- From the subconscious mind.

Profound - *adj.*
- Coming from deep within one;
- Of the greatest intensity;
- Showing intellectual penetration or emotional depths; from the depths of your being.

Inconveniences - *noun*
- An inconvenient circumstance or thing;
- Something that causes discomfort, trouble etc.
- To put to inconvenience or trouble; inco mmode.

Decency - *noun*
- The state or quality of being decent.
- Conformity to the recognized standard of propriety, goodtaste, modesty, etc.

Constructive Criticism

Deem - *verb*
- Keep in mind or convey as a conviction or view

Logic - *noun*
- Reasoned and reasonable judgment; a system of reasoning; the principles that guide reasoning within a given field or situation.

Defensive - *adj.*
- Intended or appropriate for defending against or deterring aggression or attack; *noun* an attitude of defensiveness (especially in the phrase `on the defensive').

Critiques - *noun*
- A serious examination and judgment of something; *verb* appraise critically.

Fears: the Pros & Cons

Tendency - *noun*
- A general direction in which something tends to move; an inclination to do something

Jeopardize - *verb*
- Put at risk; pose a threat to; present a danger to

Instance - *noun*
- an item of information that is representative of a type; an occurrence of something;
- *verb* clarify by giving an example of

Stems – *verb*
- To arise or originate:

Trauma - *noun*
- An emotional wound or shock often having long-lasting effects; any physical damage to the body caused by violence or accident or fracture etc.

Reversing The Hustle

Generate - *verb*
- Bring into existence; produce (energy); give or supply

Contrary - *adj.*
- Of words or propositions so related that both cannot be true but both may be false;
- exact opposition; a relation of direct opposition.

Learning to Appreciate

Appreciate - *verb*
- Increase the value of; gain in value; be fully aware of; realize fully; recognize with gratitude; be grateful for; hold dear.

Sober - *adj.*
- completely lacking in playfulness.

Newfound - *adj.*
- Newly discovered.

Your Presentation Game

Shortcoming - *noun*
- A failing or deficiency

Presentation - *noun*
- A show or display; the act of presenting something to sight or view; a visual representation of something

Internal - *adj.*
- Occurring within an institution or community; located inward; inside the country; innermost or essential.

Consist - *verb*
- Be composed of.
- be consistent in form, tenor, or character; be congruous; have its essential be.
- Comprised or contained in; be embodied in; originate (in).

Mannerisms - *noun*
- A deliberate pretense or exaggerated display; a behavioral attribute that is distinctive and peculiar to an individual.

Articulate - *adj.*
- Expressing yourself easily or characterized by clear expressive language.
- *verb* express or state clearly; speak, pronounce, or utter in a certain way; put into words or an expression.

Upping *adverb*
- To, toward, or at an elevated place on or in

Verbiage - *noun*
- Overabundance of words; the manner in which something is expressed in words.

Values and Principles

Values - *noun*
- Beliefs of a person or social group in which they have an emotional investment (either for or against something).

Instill - *verb*
- Impart gradually; fill, as with a certain quality; teach and impress by frequent repetitions or admonitions; produce or try to produce a vivid impression of.

Cues – *noun*
- A hint; intimation; guiding suggestion.

Distorted - *adj.*
- Having an intended meaning altered or misrepresented; so badly formed or out of shape as to be ugly; strained or wrenched out of normal shape.

Midst - *noun*
- The position of anything surrounded by Other things or parts, or occurring in the middle of aperiod of time, course of action, etc. (usually preceded by *the*).

Adopting New Values

Extract - *noun*
- A passage selected from a larger work;
- *verb* remove, usually with some force or effort.

Accordance - *noun*
- The act of granting rights; concurrence of opinion.

Fictional - *adj.*
- Formed or conceived by the imagination.

Reboot - *verb*
- Cause to load (an operating system) and start the initial processes

Pride: The Pros and Cons

Progression - *noun*
- A series with a definite pattern of advance; the act of moving forward toward a goal; a movement forward.

Sustained - *adj.*
- Maintained at length without interruption or weakening.

Derived - *adj.*
- Formed or developed from something else; not original.

Trait - *noun*
- A distinguishing feature of your personal nature.

Mediocrity - *noun*
- Ordinariness as a consequence of being average and not outstanding; a person of second-rate ability or value.

Ethic - *noun*
- The principles of right and wrong that are accepted by an individual or a social group; a system of principles governing morality and acceptable conduct.

Inherently - *adv.*
- In an inherent manner.

Boastful - *adj.*
- Exhibiting self-importance

Unrealistically - *adv.*
- In an unrealistic manner

Empathy - *noun*
- the psychological identification with or vicarious experiencing of the feelings, thoughts, or attitudes of another.

People, Places & Things

Embedded - *verb*
- to incorporate or contain as an essential part or characteristic.

Jeopardize - *verb*
- to put in jeopardy; hazard; risk; imperil.

Ballin' On A Budget

Priority - *noun*
- Status established in order of importance or urgency.

Pension - *noun*
- a fixed amount, other than wages, paid at regular intervals to a person or person's surviving dependents inconsideration of past services, age, merit, poverty, injury or loss sustained, etc.

401(k) *noun*
- a savings plan that allows employees to c ontribute a fixedamount of income to a re tirement account and to defer taxesuntil withdrawal.

Surplus - *noun*
- something that remains above what is used or needed.
- an amount, quantity, etc., greater than needed.

An Obligation to Change

Obligation - *noun*
- A personal relation in which one is indebted for a service or favor.
- The state of being obligated to do or pay something.

Mayhem - *noun*
- Violent and needless disturbance

Plague - *noun*
- An annoyance; any large scale calamity; *verb* annoy continually or chronically; cause to suffer a blight.

Idolize - *verb*
- Love unquestioningly and uncritically or to excess .

Leaving a Legacy

Legacy - *noun*
- Something that happened in the past or that comes from someone in the past.

Sibling - *noun*
- A person's brother or sister

Excellence - *noun*
- Possessing good qualities in high degree.
- Something in which something or someone excels.

Testament - *noun*
- A profession of belief; strong evidence for something.

Heirlooms noun
- a family possession handed down from g eneration to generation.

Mementos noun
- an object or item that serves to remind one of a person, pastevent, etc.; keepsake; souvenir.

Time Management

Forefront - *noun*
- The position of greatest importance or advancement; the leading position in any movement or field
-

Constraint - *noun*
- The state of being physically constrained; a device that retards something's motion

Incorporate - *adj.*
- Formed or united into a whole.
- *verb* unite or merge with something already in existence; include or contain; make into a whole or make part of a whole.

Structured - *adj.*
- Having definite and highly organized structure.

Building a Support System

Initial - *adj.*
- Occurring at the beginning.
- *noun* the first letter of a word (especially a person's name).

Overwhelm - *verb*
- Charge someone with too many tasks;
- Overcome, as with emotions or by superior force.

Discouraged - *adj.*
- Lacking in resolution; made less hopeful or enthusiastic.

Incarcerated On Paper

Afoul – *adverb*
- In conflict or difficulty with

Foreseeable - *adj.*
- Capable of being anticipated

Escalate - *verb*
- Increase in extent or intensity

Creating A New Game Plan

Flexible - *adj.*
- Capable of being changed.
- Making or willing to make concessions.
- Able to adjust to different conditions.

Objective - *adj.*
- The goal intended to be attained (and which is believed to be attainable)

Aspect - *noun*
- a characteristic to be considered; a distinct feature or element in a problem.
-

Implementation - *noun*
- The act of implementing (providing a practical means for accomplishing something).
- Carrying into effect; the act of accomplishing some aim or executing some order

Notes to Myself

Notes to Myself

Notes to Myself

Reentry Resources

List of Felon Friendly Employers (Companies that hire felons)
This list below is a starting point for seeking employment when you leave prison. The companies listed below are known to offer jobs to formerly incarcerated, however, does not guarantee that you will be able to land a job there. You will have to check out their hiring website, do the research and follow the application process like normal.

AAMCO Transmissions	Black and Decker	Delta Faucets
Abbott Laboratories	Blue Cross/Blue Shield	Denny's Inc.
Ace Hardware	Boeing	Dollar Rent A Car
Alamo Rent a Car	Bridgestone/Firestone	Dole Foods
Alaska Airlines	British Airways	Domino's Pizza
Alberto-Culver	Budget Rent-A-Car	Dow Brands
Allstate Insurance	Calvin Klein	Dunkin Donuts
Allstate Insurance	Campbell Soups	Dunlop Tires
America West Air	Canon USA	DuPont Co.
American Airlines	Career Education Group	Duracell
American Express	Carrier	Eddie Bauer
American Greetings	Casio, Inc.	Epson
Anderson Windows	Caterpillar	Equity Office Property Exelon
AON Computer	Chase Bank	Exxon
Archer Daniel's Midland	Chicago Mercantile Exchange	Federal Express
ARCO	Cintas	First Health Group
Arthur J. Gallagher & Co	Circuit City	Fortune Brands
AT&T	Coldwell Banker	Fruit of the Loom
Atlas Van Lines	Compaq Computer	Fuji
Avis Rent-A-Car	ConAgra Foods	General Electric
Avon Products	Dairy Queen	General Growth Properties
Baskin-Robbins	DAP Products	General Mills
Baxter International	Deer & Co	GMAC
Best Foods	Del Monte Foods	Hanes Hosiery
Best Western	Dell Corporation	Hewitt associates
BF Goodrich	Delta Air Lines	Hilton Hotels

IBM	Telephone & Data Systems	Chrysler
Illinois Tool Works	Tellabs	Comcast
Kraft Foods	Toys R Us	Comfort Inn &Suites
K-Mart	Tribune Co	Darden Restaurants
L.A. Times	U.S Cellular	Dart Containers
McDonalds	Uneven Investments	Deer Park Spring Water co.
Mobil Oil	United Airlines	Divizio Industries
Molex	Verizon	Dollar Tree
Navistar International	W.W Grainger	Dr Pepper/Seven Up
Motorola	Walgreens	Electrolux
New York Times	Wal-Mart	Embassy Suites
Newsweek	Wrigley Co	Equity Office Properties
Niki	Zebra Technologies Group	ERMCO, Inc.
Nisource	Zenith Electronics	Fairfield Inn
Northern Trust	Zerox	Florilli Transportation, LLC
Old Republic	AirTran	Flying J
Packaging Corp of America	Albertson's	Food Services of America
PACTIV	American Greetings	Galuoub Toys
Pepsi-Co	American National Logistics	Genentech
Phillip Morris	Applebee's	Golden Corral
R.R Donnelley	Aramark Food Services	Goodwill
Rubbermaid Inc.	Bahama Breeze	Great Clips
Sara-Lee	Bally's Hotel & Casino	Hampton Inn
Sears & Roebuck	Bed, Bath & Beyond	Hawthorn Suites
Service Master	Borgata Casino & Spa	HH Gregg
Seven Up, Inc.	Braum's Inc.	Hilton Hotels
Shell Oil	Brunswick Corp	Holiday Inn
Showtime Networks	Buffalo Wild Wings	Home Depot
Smurfit-Stone Container Corp	Candlewood Suites	Ikea
Sony Southwest Air	Cambell's Soup	Jack in the Box
Sprint	Carl's Jr.	Jiffy Lube
Target	Chipotle	Jimmy Johns

Kelly Moore Paints

KFC

Kohl's

Labor Ready

Lowes

Luby's Maggiano's

Marriott Hotels

Men's Wearhouse

Metals USA

Miller Brewing Company

Nordstrom

O'Charleys

OIX, Inc.

Old Republic International

Olive Garden

Omni Direct

Pappadeaux

Party City

Perkins Restaurants

PetSmart

Radisson

Red Lobster

Red Robin

Residence Inn

Restaurant Depot

Reyes Beverage Group

Ross

RSC Equipment Rental

Revel Hotel Resort & Casino

Safeway

Salvation Army

Sharaton Hotels

Shoprite Simplex Leasing

Sisbro, Inc.

Springhill Suites

Starwood Hotels

Subway

Sysco

Teleperformance

TGI Friday

Towneplace Suites

Trader Joes

Tradewinds

Tribune Company

Tyson Foods

Uhaul

UPS

US Steel Corporation

Voyager Express, Inc

Wendy's

Wm. Wrigley Jr. Company

Wyndham Hotels

Xerox

WinCo Foods

Yard House

RESOURCES, INFORMATION & ASSISTANCE

The following web sites have great resource information to help you prepare for your release, whatever your needs are.

http://www.hirenetwork.org/clearinghouse

http://www.helpforfelons.org/reentry-programs-ex-offenders-state/

http://csgjusticecenter.org/reentry/reentry-services-directory/

http://insidebooksproject.org/resource-guide/

http://www.urban.org/policy-centers/justice-policy-center

http://johnjayresearch.org/pri/

http://www.reentry.net/ny/

http://www.csosa.gov/reentry/resources.aspx

http://www.bop.gov/inmates/custody_and_care/reentry.jsp

BEYOND PRISON PROBATION AND PAROLE

A film series

Beyond Prison, Probation & Parole is a motivational film series that features inspiring stories told by formerly incarcerated men and women who have overcome the hurdles, stigmas, and challenges associated with returning to society from prison. For many people, getting out of prison can feel like an insurmountable task but there are some who come home and go on to become successful and productive citizens.

In Beyond Prison Probation & Parole these individuals not only share their recipes for success, they also tell how they refused to let their past dictate their future. This film series is a low-cost, high-value approach to reducing the prison recidivism rate by proving success is attainable after incarceration. Each feature in the series uses motivational engagement as a powerful tool to energize, inspire and of course motivate people who want and need to transition from a life of poor choices, substance abuse and criminal behavior, to a positive and productive life.

"Prison is not bad for everybody. For some people, prison can give them a purpose in life." **Terrence Jeffries**

"Prison sits you down and forces you to evaluate all the decisions that got you there." **Jm Benjamin**"

"I was hanging on to a thread and I knew I had to get it together." **Lourdes Cartegena**

"Prison is like a university, a place you can learn how to better yourself, if you take the necessary time to study yourself." **Anthony McFadden**

"When I was incarcerated, my whole family was incarcerated. I left a young daughter without a father." **Danny Gonzalez**

"When I got my GED in prison I knew I was on the road to a better life, and that was just the beginning." **Terry L Wroten**

For more info to purchase visit www.reentrystrategies.com

Changin' Your Game Plan

How I used Incarceration as a stepping-stone for SUCCESS

Non-Fiction
ISBN#
Paperback 5 ½ by 8 ½
252 Pages,

Randy Kearse spent over 30 years of his life incarcerated in some shape form or fashion. From the age of 17 to 50 Randy was either in jail, prison, on probation, parole or on the run from law enforcement. The judge called Mr. Kearse a menace before sentencing him to 15 years in prison.

Entering prison at 27 and not getting out until 40, Mr. Kearse knew he had to make some drastic changes if he wanted to successfully transition from prison back to society, his family and community.

Changin' Your Game Plan: How I used incarceration as a stepping stone for SUCCESS is about Randy's journey of change, and that's exactly what it was, a journey. He walks readers through the struggles, internal conflicts and challenges one faces when he or she decides to leave the street mentality alone and embrace change. Changin' Your Game Plan is an inspiring story of one man's determination to put the past behind him and reinvent a better future himself.

"Randy Kearse is an inspiration to disenfranchised men and women from all walks of life. Overcoming the challenges, stigmas and obstacles after prison isn't easy."

Marguerite Spence

Randy Kearse, author, filmmaker, TV talk show host, motivational speaker and prison reentry consultant spent 30 years of life incarcerated in one shape, form, or fashion. He has successfully mapped a way out of the negative mindsets and negative behavioral patterns, which send so many people back and forth to prison. Mr. Kearse shows you how to break free from the mental incarceration that led to his physical incarceration.

Make Check/Money Order:
Reentry Strategies - 1 West Prospect Ave #155, Mt. Vernon, NY 10550!

Name_____

Inmate Reg.#_____

Address_____

City, State, ZipCode_____

Changin' Your Game Plan $15.00 (per copy) S&H $2.99 (per copy) Total _____ _____

Order Online www.reentrystrategies.com   email: reentrystrategies@gmail.com

Changin' Your Game Plan

The Blueprint for SUCCESSFUL Prison Reentry

Prison Reentry Readiness Workbook
ISBN# 978-0-9800974-7-4
Paperback 8 ½ by 11 ½
252 Pages, 50+ Chapters
w/questions
Vocabulary building
Reentry resources

The Changin' Your Game Plan workbook is a prison reentry readiness study guide. At 252 pages, it has 50+ soul searching chapters, and questions that bring the reader face-to-face with there own personal truths. It's a practical approach to change, doing time and successfully transitioning back to one's family, community and life in a positive and productive way.

One's "Game Plan" is the goals and plans he or she make for their life. Change in thinking, behaviors and attitudes are part of the process to creating a new game plan. Changing one's game plan will greatly increase the chances of not only successfully transitioning back to society, but also increase one's chances of staying out or prison.

Changin' Your Game Plan is not based on prison reentry *theory* or based on a set of *thoughtless ideas* developed by a nameless official tucked away in a comfortable office somewhere, who doesn't have a clue what the day to day struggles are for someone who is not only getting out of prison physically, but, someone who has to breakout of the mental prison he or she has been living in (for some almost half their life).

"After the Bible or Koran, Chnagin' Your Game Plan is a must have for your incarcerated son, daughter, mother, father, sibling, uncle, aunt, cousin (distant and play cousin), child's father or mother, or long lost friend."
Anthony McFadden. Reentry Specialist

Randy Kearse, author, filmmaker, tv talk show host, motivational speaker and prison reentry consultant spent 30 years of life incarcerated in one shape, form or fashion. He has successfully mapped a way out of the negative mindsets and negative behavioral patterns, which send so many people back and forth to prison. Mr. Kearse shows you how to break free from the mental incarceration that led to his physical incarceration.

Make Check/Money Order:
Reentry Strategies - 1 West Prospect Ave #155, Mt. Vernon, NY 10550

Name_____

Inmate Reg.#_____

Address_____

City, State, ZipCode_____

Changin' Your Game Plan $29.99 (per copy) S&H $2.99 (per copy)   Total _____

Order Online www.reentrystrategies.com   email: reentrystrategies@gmail.com

Made in the USA
Lexington, KY
16 April 2017